FINANCIAL INSTITUTIONS AND SERVICES

FINANCIAL MARKET UTILITIES AND KEY FINANCIAL MARKET INFRASTRUCTURE ELEMENTS

Financial Institutions and Services

Additional books in this series can be found on Nova's website under the Series tab.

Additional E-books in this series can be found on Nova's website under the E-book tab.

FINANCIAL INSTITUTIONS AND SERVICES

FINANCIAL MARKET UTILITIES AND KEY FINANCIAL MARKET INFRASTRUCTURE ELEMENTS

JOVAN BARANK
EDITOR

NOVINKA
New York

For permission to use material from this book please contact us:
Telephone 631-231-7269; Fax 631-231-8175
Web Site: http://www.novapublishers.com

Library of Congress Cataloging-in-Publication Data

ISBN: 978-1-62618-052-9

Published by Nova Science Publishers, Inc. † New York

CONTENTS

Preface		**vii**
Chapter 1	Supervision of U.S. Payment, Clearing, and Settlement Systems: Designation of Financial Market Utilities (FMUs) *Marc Labonte*	**1**
Chapter 2	Financial Market Utilities: A Rule by the Federal Reserve System *Board of Governors of the Federal Reserve System*	**45**
Chapter 3	The Dodd-Frank Wall Street Reform and Consumer Protection Act: Title VII, Derivatives *Rena S. Miller and Kathleen Ann Ruane*	**87**
Index		**117**

PREFACE

The U.S. financial system processes millions of transactions each day representing daily transfers of trillions of dollars, securities, and other assets to facilitate purchases and payments. Concerns had been raised, even prior to the recent financial crisis, about the vulnerability of the U.S. financial system to infrastructure failure. These concerns about the "plumbing" of the financial system were heightened following the market disruptions of the recent crisis. This book outlines the changes to the supervision of key market infrastructure that are embodied in the Dodd-Frank Act, and how the associated systems are currently overseen and regulated.

Chapter 1 - The U.S. financial system processes millions of transactions each day representing daily transfers of trillions of dollars, securities, and other assets to facilitate purchases and payments. Concerns had been raised, even prior to the recent financial crisis, about the vulnerability of the U.S. financial system to infrastructure failure. These concerns about the “plumbing” of the financial system were heightened following the market disruptions of the recent crisis.

The financial market infrastructure consists of the various systems, networks, and technological processes that are necessary for conducting and completing financial transactions. Title VIII of the Dodd-Frank Act, P.L. 111-203, the Payment, Clearing, and Settlement Supervision Act of 2010, introduces the term “financial market utility” (FMU or utility) for those multilateral systems that transfer, clear, or settle payments, securities, or other financial transactions among financial institutions (FI) or between an FMU and a financial institution. Utilities and FIs transfer funds and settle accounts with other financial institutions to facilitate normal day-to-day transactions occurring in the U.S. economy. Those transfers include payroll and mortgage payments, foreign currency exchanges, purchases of U.S. treasury bonds and corporate securities, and derivatives trades. Further, financial institutions engage in commercial paper and securities repurchase agreements (repo) markets that contribute to liquidity in the U.S. economy. In the United States, some of the key payment, clearing, and settlement (PCS) systems are operated by the Federal Reserve, and other systems are operated by private sector organizations.

Chapter 2 - The Board is publishing a final rule, Regulation HH, Designated Financial Market Utilities. This rule implements provisions of sections 805(a) and 806(e) of the Dodd-Frank Wall Street Reform and Consumer Protection Act ("Dodd-Frank Act" or "Act"), including risk-management standards for financial market utilities ("FMUs") that are designated as systemically important by the Financial Stability Oversight Council (the "Council") and standards for determining when a designated FMU is required to provide advance notice of proposed changes to its rules, procedures, or operations that could materially affect the nature or level of risks presented by the designated FMU.

Chapter 3 - The financial crisis implicated the over-the-counter (OTC) derivatives market as a major source of systemic risk. A number of firms used derivatives to construct highly leveraged speculative positions, which generated enormous losses that threatened to bankrupt not only the firms themselves but also their creditors and trading partners. Hundreds of billions of dollars in government credit were needed to prevent such losses from cascading throughout the system. AIG was the best-known example, but by no means the only one.

Equally troublesome was the fact that the OTC market depended on the financial stability of a dozen or so major dealers. Failure of a dealer would have resulted in the nullification of trillions of dollars worth of contracts and would have exposed derivatives counterparties to sudden risk and loss, exacerbating the cycle of deleveraging and withholding of credit that characterized the crisis. During the crisis, all the major dealers came under stress, and even though derivatives dealing was not generally the direct source of financial weakness, a collapse of the $600 trillion OTC derivatives market was imminent absent federal intervention. The first group of Troubled Asset Relief Program (TARP) recipients included nearly all the large derivatives dealers.

In: Financial Market Utilities ...
Editor: Jovan Barank

ISBN: 978-1-62618-052-9

Chapter 1

SUPERVISION OF U.S. PAYMENT, CLEARING, AND SETTLEMENT SYSTEMS: DESIGNATION OF FINANCIAL MARKET UTILITIES (FMUs)*

Marc Labonte

SUMMARY

The U.S. financial system processes millions of transactions each day representing daily transfers of trillions of dollars, securities, and other assets to facilitate purchases and payments. Concerns had been raised, even prior to the recent financial crisis, about the vulnerability of the U.S. financial system to infrastructure failure. These concerns about the "plumbing" of the financial system were heightened following the market disruptions of the recent crisis.

The financial market infrastructure consists of the various systems, networks, and technological processes that are necessary for conducting and completing financial transactions. Title VIII of the Dodd-Frank Act, P.L. 111-203, the Payment, Clearing, and Settlement Supervision Act of 2010, introduces the term "financial market utility" (FMU or utility) for those multilateral systems that transfer, clear, or settle payments, securities, or other financial transactions among financial institutions (FI) or between an FMU and a financial institution. Utilities and FIs transfer

* This is an edited, reformatted and augmented version of a Congressional Research Service publication, CRS Report for Congress R41529, prepared for Members and Committees of Congress, from www.crs.gov, dated September 10, 2012.

funds and settle accounts with other financial institutions to facilitate normal day-to-day transactions occurring in the U.S. economy. Those transfers include payroll and mortgage payments, foreign currency exchanges, purchases of U.S. treasury bonds and corporate securities, and derivatives trades. Further, financial institutions engage in commercial paper and securities repurchase agreements (repo) markets that contribute to liquidity in the U.S. economy. In the United States, some of the key payment, clearing, and settlement (PCS) systems are operated by the Federal Reserve, and other systems are operated by private sector organizations.

With Title VIII of the Dodd-Frank Act, which was enacted on July 21, 2010, Congress added a new regulatory framework for the FMUs and PCS activities (of FIs) designated by the Financial Stability Oversight Council as systemically important.

On July 18, 2012, the Council voted unanimously to designate eight FMUs as systemically important. Title VIII expands the Federal Reserve's role, in coordination with those of other prudential regulators, in the supervision, examination, and rule enforcement with respect to those FMUs and PCS activities of financial institutions. Additionally, FMUs may borrow from the discount window of the Federal Reserve in certain unusual and exigent circumstances.

Although Title VIII primarily affects the scope of regulatory powers, certain provisions directly affect a utility's business operations. For example, Title VIII allows FMUs to maintain accounts at a Federal Reserve Bank and provides access to the Fed's discount window in unusual and exigent circumstances.

Related to PCS, Title VII of the Dodd-Frank Act imposes requirements that will significantly affect the business of clearinghouses in the over-the-counter (OTC) derivatives (swaps) market. By requiring clearing of certain swap transactions through central counterparties (CCPs or clearinghouses), Title VII is expected to increase the volume of transactions processed by clearing systems subject to Title VIII.

Critics contend that Title VIII grants too much discretionary authority to the Fed in an area that they argue was not a source of systemic risk during the recent financial crisis. S. 3497 seeks to repeal Title VIII of the Dodd-Frank Act, stripping FSOC of it's authority to designate FMUs as systemically important.

This report outlines the changes to the supervision of key market infrastructure that are embodied in the Dodd-Frank Act. It is intended to be used as a reference for those interested in the financial system's "plumbing," and how the associated systems are currently overseen and regulated.

INTRODUCTION

On July 21, 2010, Title VIII of the Dodd-Frank Act,[1] the *Payment, Clearing, and Settlement Supervision Act of 2010*, became effective upon enactment. Title VIII authorizes the Federal Reserve, in coordination with other federal agencies, to supervise and regulate the infrastructure that enables financial intermediaries to process and complete financial transactions.

Payment, clearing, and settlement (PCS) activities facilitate a variety of financial transactions such as transferring payments for and completing retail purchases, foreign exchange transactions, securities transactions, and derivatives trades. Some key systems in the United States have been operated by the Federal Reserve Banks and others by the private sector. PCS systems serve a critical role in the financial services sector and the broader economy. In the United States, the value of transactions for large-value payment systems amounted to $1.06 quadrillion in 2011.[2]

Attention was drawn to the functioning of the U.S. financial system in 2008 when major financial institutions entered bankruptcy (e.g., Lehman Brothers), receivership (e.g., Washington Mutual), or were kept solvent through government assistance (e.g., AIG). The interconnectedness of large financial intermediaries deemed "too-big-to-fail" heightened concerns about systemic risk, which can be understood as the failure of one firm leading to system-wide disruptions. One channel through which systemic risk can spread, as discussed in this report, is a disruption, such as the failure of a "too-big-to-fail" institution, cascading through PCS systems or activities.

AIG, a major insurance company, experienced a crisis stemming from a subsidiary that was a leading underwriter of credit default swaps (CDS), a type of over-the-counter derivative.[3] CDS provide protection to buyers against credit events such as an issuer's default on corporate debt obligations and structured securities. CDS had been traded bilaterally between institutions through an over-the-counter market system that regulatory authorities had criticized for its inefficiencies and lack of transparency. The Federal Reserve Bank of New York undertook efforts to encourage industry participants to voluntarily improve the infrastructure of the OTC derivatives market in recent years. In 2006, Alan Greenspan, then-Chairman of the Federal Reserve, reportedly said that he was appalled that people were relying on scraps of paper to record transactions, a practice which some blamed for causing a backlog of unconfirmed contracts.[4]

Prior to the Dodd-Frank Act, various federal regulatory authorities had oversight responsibilities for certain systems or entities engaged in processing those financial transactions. Title VIII reflects recommendations by the previous and current administrations to give the Federal Reserve explicit statutory oversight authority with respect to elements of the financial infrastructure in the United States, while also giving similar authority to the Securities and Exchange Commission (SEC) and Commodity Futures Trading Commission (CFTC) for certain parts of the infrastructure. Title VIII introduces the term "financial market utility" (FMU or utility) for those multilateral systems that transfer, clear, or settle payments, securities, or other financial transactions among financial institutions (FI) or between a FMU and a financial institution. Title VIII addresses the federal regulatory oversight of systemically important payment, clearing, and settlement (PCS) systems and PCS activities of financial institutions that facilitate various financial transactions. Financial transactions processed daily in the U.S. economy include payment transfers ranging from small-dollar retail purchase transactions to large-value purchases of securities; clearing transactions for derivatives trading; and securities settlement.

Title VIII regulatory powers apply specifically to those financial market utilities and PCS activities (of financial institutions) that are designated as systemically important by the Financial Stability Oversight Council (FSOC), also created by the Dodd-Frank Act. It is notable that Title VIII does not consolidate or centralize authority for the approval of the formation of new utilities or PCS activities with the Federal Reserve or any single regulatory agency. Prior to the enactment of Title VIII, the Federal Reserve derived its oversight responsibilities for payment and settlement systems from a range of statutory responsibilities for monetary policy, banking supervision, lender of last resort, and provision of payment and settlement services.[5] Recently, the Federal Reserve released a final rule regarding FMUs.[6] On July 18, 2012, FSOC voted unanimously to designate eight FMUs as systemically important (see "FMUs Designated by the FSOC"). FSOC did not designate any PCS activities as systemically important at that time. Title VIII primarily addresses the regulatory framework rather than affecting the flows of funds through existing payment and settlement systems. TitleVII addresses the derivatives clearing systems and activities for OTC swap transactions. [7]

Some Representatives opposed Title VIII and struck the title governing PCS supervision from the financial reform bill that the House of Representatives passed in December 2009. Concerns held by some opponents of the title may have included a sense that the U.S. financial infrastructure was adequately supervised, or that the title might have given too much discretionary authority to the Federal Reserve. Other reservations may have included the view that Title VIII was unnecessary in light of the Federal Reserve's efforts to encourage firms to voluntarily strengthen infrastructure procedures in various markets, and the absence of a PCS-related breakdown in September 2008. S. 3497, introduced on August 2, 2012, seeks to repeal Title VIII, stripping FSOC of its authority to designate FMUs as systemically important. This report begins by introducing the major PCS systems operating in the United States, followed by the basics of PCS systems and activities. The report then describes the different risks, including systemic risk, that are commonly associated with PCS systems and activities. The next part of the report discusses the oversight authority of the FMU and FI regulators that was in place prior to the enactment of the Dodd-Frank Act, after which the report summarizes the changes made by Title VIII, including the new regulatory oversight authority of the Fed. The final part of the report addresses implementation of Title VIII by relevant agencies and the impact of Title VIII on FMUs and FIs.

Major Payment, Clearing, and Settlement Systems in the United States

The Federal Reserve and the private sector operate the systems that constitute the infrastructure for the processing and completion of financial transactions in the United States. Listed below are some of the major systems currently operating in the United States. Some privately-operated systems have been designated by FSOC as systemically important under Title VIII. Additional information regarding selected systems, including recent transaction volume levels, is set forth in an *Appendix* to this report. In the future, new and evolving types of financial products, transactions and instruments could lead to new payment, clearing, and settlement systems and activities.

FMUs Designated by the FSOC

On July 18, 2012, FSOC voted unanimously to designate eight FMUs as systemically important. Each was assigned a supervisory agency on the basis of the types of activities that they perform. The eight systemically important FMUs are:

- The Clearing House Payments Company, on the basis of its role as operator of the Clearing House Interbank Payments System (CHIPS).[8] *(Supervisory Agency—The Federal Reserve)*
- CLS Bank (foreign exchange) (Supervisory Agency—The Federal Reserve)
- Chicago Mercantile Exchange (CME) Clearing (credit default and interest rate swaps) (Supervisory Agency—Commodity Futures Trading Commission)
- Depository Trust Company (DTC) (Supervisory Agency—Securities and Exchange Commission)
- Fixed Income Clearing Corporation operating the Government Securities Division (GSD) and the Mortgage-Backed Securities Division (MBSD) (Supervisory Agency—Securities and Exchange Commission)
- ICE Trust (credit default swaps) (Supervisory Agency—Commodity Futures Trading Commission) National Securities Clearing Corporation (NSCC) (Supervisory Agency—Securities and Exchange Commission
- The Options Clearing Corporation (equity derivatives) (Supervisory Agency—Securities and Exchange Commission)

The Clearing House operates an interbank funds transfer system known as CHIPS and an ACH system known as EPN. DTCC operates the Depository Trust Company (DTC), the major U.S. depository, and clearing corporations for government, mortgage-backed, and corporate and municipal securities. These entities provide the primary infrastructure for the clearance, settlement, and custody of the vast majority of transactions in the United States involving equities, corporate debt, municipal bonds, money market instruments, and government securities.[9] In the future, FSOC may add or remove PCS systems from the designated list, as conditions warrant.

Systems Operated by the Federal Reserve

The Federal Reserve Banks operate the following three wholesale payment services and an electronic payment system providing ACH services to depository institutions:

- Fedwire® Funds Service
- Fedwire Securities Service, also known as the National Book-Entry System (NBES)
- National Settlement Service (NSS)
- FedACH® Service

The Federal Reserve Banks began providing services using telecommunications in the early 1900s to transfer funds between accounts maintained in different Federal Reserve Districts.[10] In 1981, the Federal Reserve was required by law to price most of the Federal Reserve Bank financial services, including funds transfers and securities safekeeping, and to give nonmember depository institutions direct access to those services.[11] The Fedwire services enable depository institutions, the U.S. Treasury and other government agencies to transfer funds and book-entry securities nationwide. The Fedwire Funds Services is a real-time gross settlement (RTGS) system to settle funds electronically between banks; the Fedwire Securities Service provides issuance, settlement, and transfer services for U.S. Treasury securities and other government-related securities; and the National Settlement Service, which is a multilateral settlement service, is used by clearinghouses, financial exchanges, and other clearing and settlement groups. The Fedwire funds and securities transactions are processed in real time when received and are final and irrevocable when settled. By increasing the efficiency of Federal Reserve open market operations and helping to keep the market for government securities liquid, the Fedwire Securities Service plays a significant role in how the Federal Reserve conducts monetary policy,[12] which is commonly understood as the regulation of the money supply and interest rates by central banks. Open market operations, which are purchases and sales of U.S. Treasury and federal agency securities, are the Federal Reserve's principal tool for implementing monetary policy.[13] When the FSOC designated the private sector FMUs in July 2012, the Fed "reaffirmed its longstanding policy of applying relevant international risk-management standards to the Federal Reserve Banks' Fedwire funds and Fedwire securities services."[14]

OTHER SYSTEMS OPERATED BY THE PRIVATE SECTOR

There are other smaller or foreign-based PCS systems that FSOC did not designate as FMUs in 2012. For example, the Depository Trust & Clearing

Corporation (DTCC) also operates other essential, though not systemically important, private-sector systems in the United States. These systems are a group of DTCC subsidiaries, which include Euro CCP, AVOX and FICC among others. Some foreign-based systems provided PCS services for U.S. financial actors. For example, the Society for Worldwide Interbank Financial Telecommunication (SWIFT) is an international financial messaging system headquartered in Belgium with U.S. operations, and LCH.Clearnet is an important clearinghouse for several categories of assets.

The *Appendix* to this report provides additional information regarding these systems.

Basics of Payment, Clearing, and Settlement

The existing infrastructure in the United States for those activities consists of systems operated by the Federal Reserve through the Federal Reserve Banks, and by the private sector. In some cases, PCS activities are conducted primarily through one central party, such as the Fed or a clearinghouse. In other cases, activities are also conducted bilaterally through two financial institutions. This section describes the definitions and functions of these systems and activities that may partly overlap.

The following types of systems and activities are covered by Title VIII:

- payment systems, which transfer funds electronically from one institution to another;
- clearing systems (or clearinghouses), which in the derivatives market often transfer credit risk to a central counterparty (CCP) (clearinghouse) from each counterparty to a trade; and
- settlement systems, which complete transactions such as securities trades.

Payment Systems

In general terms, a payment system consists of the means for transferring money between suppliers and users of funds through the use of cash substitutes such as checks, drafts, and electronic funds transfers. The Committee on Payment and Settlement Systems (CPSS), consisting of representatives from several international regulatory authorities, has developed generally accepted definitions of standard payment system terminology.[15] As defined by the CPSS, a payment system is a system that consists of a set of instruments, banking procedures, and, typically, interbank funds transfer systems that ensure the circulation of money.

In the United States, the Federal Reserve Banks and the private sector operate payment systems that process retail or wholesale transactions.[16] Retail payment systems facilitate a consumer's ability to purchase goods and services, pay bills, obtain cash through withdrawals and advances, and make person-to-person payments. Retail payments tend to generate a large number of transactions that have relatively small value per transaction and are processed through electronic funds transfer systems, including automated clearing house (ACH) transactions and debit and credit card transactions at the point of sale.[17]

The ACH is an electronic funds transfer (EFT) system that processes credit and debit transactions such as direct deposit payroll and consumer bill payments. ACH is the primary EFT system used by federal governmental agencies to make payments, according to the Financial Management Service (FMS), a bureau of the United States Department of the Treasury.[18] Providers of ACH services include the Federal Reserve Banks through the FedACH Service and The Electronic Payments Network, which is the only private-sector ACH operator in the United States.[19] Rules governing the ACH system for participating financial institutions are established by NACHA – The Electronic Payments Association, a trade association,[20] which oversees the ACH Network, and by the Federal Reserve.[21] NACHA reports that more than 20.2 billion ACH payments were made in 2011.[22]

Wholesale payment systems generally support domestic and international commercial activities and financial market related activities. Large-value, wholesale funds transfer systems are used for purchasing, selling, or financing securities transactions; disbursing or repaying loans; settling real estate transactions; and making large-value, time-critical payments (e.g., settling interbank purchases, Federal funds sales, or foreign exchange transactions).23 Wholesale payments tend to have a large per-transaction value and a relatively small number of transactions generated daily and are processed through payment systems such as the Fedwire Funds Service (Fedwire)24 and The Clearing House Interbank Payments System (CHIPS).25 Wholesale payment systems also provide final clearing and settlement for a variety of retail payment systems at the end of the business day. Financial institutions use intra-bank systems to initiate, process, and transmit large-value payment orders internally and to interface with Fedwire and CHIPS.

Clearing Systems

Clearing systems conduct various activities related to payment, currency, securities or derivatives transactions. The CPSS defines a *clearing system* as a set of procedures whereby financial institutions present and exchange data or documents relating to funds or securities transfers to other financial institutions at a single location (clearing house). The procedures often include a mechanism to facilitate the establishment of net positions of participant obligations for settlement, a process known as netting.[26] A *clearing house* is a central location or central processing mechanism through which financial institutions agree to exchange payment instructions or other financial obligations such as securities. The term *clearing*, which is the process of transmitting, reconciling and possibly confirming payment orders or security transfer instructions prior to settlement, sometimes is used imprecisely to include settlement.

Two of the major types of clearing houses in the United States process securities and derivatives transactions. For securities transactions, a clearing corporation or a depository must register with the Securities and Exchange Commission (SEC) as a clearing agency (CA).[27] Clearing corporations clear member transactions, enable automated settlement of those trades, and often act as intermediaries in making settlements. They also guarantee the completion of all transactions and interpose themselves as parties to both sides of a transaction.[28]

Depositories maintain ownership records of securities on the books of the depository, hold securities certificates (physical securities are held in vaults), and make securities deliveries for settlements requiring delivery. Currently, the Depository Trust Company (DTC) is the primary U.S. securities depository.[29] The DTC is a subsidiary of The Depository & Clearing Corporation (DTCC),[30] which also operates the Fixed Income Clearing Corporation (FICC). FICC clears government and mortgage-backed securities through its clearing corporation divisions known as the Government Securities Division (GSD) and the Mortgage-Backed Securities Division (MBSD). In addition, the National Securities Clearing Corporation (NSCC), which is a subsidiary of DTCC, is a registered clearing corporation regulated by the SEC that provides clearing and settlement services for corporate and municipal securities.

In the futures and options markets, a clearing house, known as a derivatives clearing organization (DCO), must register with the Commodity Futures Trading Commission (CFTC) to provide clearing services with respect to futures contracts and options on those futures contracts traded on a designated contract market and swap transactions traded over-the-counter.[31] A DCO enables the parties to a derivatives transaction (counterparties) to transfer credit risk to the clearing house, for example, through novation. Novation occurs when a single derivatives contract between two counterparties becomes two separate contracts: one between the clearing house and each counterparty. As of August 2012, there were 25 DCOs registered with the CFTC.[32]

Settlement Systems

The CPSS defines *settlement*, in part, as the completion of a transaction wherein the seller transfers securities or financial instruments to the buyer and the buyer transfers money to the seller. A settlement may be final or provisional. A *settlement system* is used to facilitate the settlement of transfers of funds or financial instruments. In a *real-time gross settlement system* (RTGS), processing and settling occur on an order-by-order basis in real time instead of through netting of transaction positions. A *securities settlement system* is a particular kind of settlement system that consists of the full set of institutional arrangements for confirmation, clearance and settlement of securities trades and safekeeping of securities.

In the United States, the Federal Reserve Banks and the private sector operate different settlement systems for securities transactions. Securities processing within financial institutions and the major markets accounts for the majority of large-value payments.[33]

The major securities markets in the United States include the markets for government securities, corporate equities and bonds, money market instruments, and municipal bonds. Those instruments are generally traded through organized exchanges or through over-the-counter dealer markets.[34] Depository institutions play several important roles in securities clearing and settlement. In addition to participating in clearing and settlement transactions, depository institutions act as custodians, issuing and paying agents, and settling banks for their customers.

The U.S. government securities market includes all primary and secondary market transactions in securities issued by the U.S. Treasury, certain federal government agencies, and federal government-sponsored enterprises.[35] Trading in government securities is conducted over-the-counter between brokers, dealers, and investors, which means that parties trade on a bilateral basis with one another rather than on an organized exchange. The Federal Reserve operates a book-entry system known as the National Book-Entry System, or the Fedwire Securities Service, through which nearly all U.S. government securities are issued and transferred.[36] The Fixed Income Clearing Corporation (FICC) also supports the selling and trading of U.S. government securities.

Corporations and municipal governments also issue various types of securities, including corporate equities and bonds, commercial paper,[37] and municipal bonds. Various securities are traded on established U.S. exchanges, including the New York Stock Exchange, the American Stock Exchange, and the NASDAQ system, and on over-the-counter markets. The National Securities Clearing Corporation (NSCC) provides clearing, settlement, and other services for virtually all broker-to-broker trades involving equities, corporate and municipal debt, and certain other instruments traded on over-the-counter markets and exchanges.[38]

RISKS OF PAYMENT, CLEARING, AND SETTLEMENT SYSTEMS AND ACTIVITIES

Section 802 of the Dodd-Frank Act reflects concern about risks related to PCS systems and activities. For example, the proper functioning of the financial markets is considered dependent upon safe and efficient arrangements for the clearing and settlement of payment, securities, and other financial transactions. Although financial market utilities that conduct or support multilateral PCS activities may reduce risks for their participants and the broader financial system, such utilities may also concentrate and create new risks. Congress also found that PCS activities conducted by financial institutions present risks to the participating financial institutions and to the financial system. Congress found it necessary to enhance the regulation and supervision of utilities and PCS activities that are systemically important, in part, to reduce systemic risk and to promote safety and soundness.

Further, both the Bush and Obama Administrations addressed the risks arising from payment and settlement systems in proposing financial regulatory reforms. In those proposals for heightened supervision by the Federal Reserve, the U.S. Department of the Treasury noted concerns about the ability of payment and settlement systems to contribute to financial crises, rather than reduce them, potentially threatening the stability of U.S. and foreign financial markets.[39]

Systemic Risk

There is no single definition of systemic risk. The Federal Reserve Bank of Cleveland has indicated that a firm is considered systemically important if its failure would have economically significant spillover effects which, if left unchecked, could destabilize the financial system and have a negative impact on the real economy.[40] In order to provide more guidance in practice, however, the Cleveland Fed proposes using the following four factors, other than size, for designating firms as systemically important: contagion, correlation, concentration, and conditions (context). The International Monetary Fund summarizes systemic risk as the large losses to other financial institutions induced by the failure of a particular interconnected institution.[41] Congress has addressed systemic risk in a number of provisions of the Dodd-Frank Act, in part, through the establishment of the Financial Stability Oversight Council and the regulation of systemically significant firms.[42]

Systemic risk can be increased by the transmission of financial system disruptions through payment and settlement systems. The global payment and settlement infrastructure consists of a network of domestic and cross-border systems that are increasingly connected through a wide array of complex interrelationships.[43] Financial market utilities, financial institutions, and other system participants are increasingly connected as operators of and participants in such systems.

Payment and settlement risks have the potential to impose losses on the entity at the source of a disruption as well as on its direct counterparties or customers, and in some circumstances, their counterparties or customers.[44] Financial institutions engage in a range of financial activities that require the settlement of obligations and transfer of assets, which can lead to principal credit losses or replacement costs when these transfers do not occur as expected.[45] The entity that is the source of an initial credit, liquidity or operational disruption, such as a fail ed securities trade or operational outage, may face lost revenue. That entity's customers and counterparties may face replacement costs from the purchase of additional funds or securities at a potentially higher market price to complete their own obligations. A settlement institution may also redistribute payment and settlement risks back to its participants through loss-sharing arrangements that may apply to participants that had no transactions with the failing entity. Further, some types of interdependencies among systems can allow an initial disruption to activate a chain of different risks and transmit an initial disruption through multiple systems. The interdependencies of financial intermediaries thus increase the potential for disruptions to spread quickly and widely, including across multiple systems. Several factors over the past few decades have contributed to the development of such interdependencies.[46] These factors include the globalization and regional integration of the financial sector, consolidation of financial institutions, and advances in computer and telecommunications technology. Events during the financial crisis of 2008 included the transmission of disruptions arising from the failure of large, interconnected financial institutions through payment, clearing, and settlement systems. In the view of some international banking regulators, the financial market infrastructures generally performed well during the recent financial crisis and did much to help prevent the crisis from becoming even more serious.[47] Those regulators have argued that when robust financial market infrastructures can enable settlement to take place without significant counterparty risk, such systems help markets to remain liquid even during times of financial stress.[48]

Some observers argue that another source of systemic risk could be the clearing house that functions as a central counterparty, i.e., the buyer to every seller and the seller to every buyer, in derivatives transactions.[49] That risk arguably could increase because of the Title VII provisions requiring the clearing of swaps transactions under certain circumstances. In addition, academics are studying whether the use of central clearing counterparties actually reduces counterparty risk.[50] In Title VIII, Congress indicated that financial market utilities may also concentrate and create new risks and stated that such utilities must be well designed and operated in a safe and sound manner.[51]

Other Risks

In addition to systemic risk, the Federal Reserve has identified the following four basic risks in payment and settlement systems:

- *credit risk*, which is the risk that a counterparty will not settle an obligation for full value either when due, or anytime thereafter;
- *liquidity risk*, which is the risk that a counterparty will not settle an obligation for full value when due;
- *operational risk*, which is the risk of loss resulting from inadequate or failed internal processes, people, and systems, or from external events, and which includes various physical and information security risks; and
- *legal risk,* which is the risk of loss because of the unexpected application of a law or regulation or because a contract cannot be enforced.[52]

These risks can, but need not, lead to systemic risk. Due to the potential for significant loss resulting from the large dollar value of wholesale payments, regulators expect financial institutions to implement effective and appropriate risk management policies, procedures, and controls to protect against such risks as well as reputation and strategic risk.[53] Institutions involved with wholesale payments must also manage legal and compliance risk under laws administered by the Office of Foreign Assets Control imposing economic sanctions against specified foreign countries and individuals and by the record-keeping and reporting requirements of the Bank Secrecy Act, as amended by the USA PATRIOT Act.[54]

Operational risks arising from wholesale payments include risks relating to internal and operational controls, audit, information security, business continuity planning, and vendor and third-party management. Security risk may arise from intra-bank funds transfers. A financial institution's funds transfer operation, often known as "the wire room," is responsible for originating, transmitting, and receiving payment orders. Financial institutions must establish the authenticity of incoming and outgoing funds transfer messages and the time of receipt of incoming payment orders.[55]

Regulatory Oversight Prior to Title VIII

Recommendations to Strengthen Oversight

Prior to Title VIII, an entity's supervisory agency, and for certain entities, the Federal Reserve, conducted prudential oversight of payment, clearing, and settlement systems and activities of financial institutions.[56] The Federal Reserve relied on "a patchwork of authorities, largely derived from [its] role as a banking supervisor, as well as on moral suasion" as a means to help ensure that payment and settlement systems had necessary procedures and controls in place to manage their risks.[57] In 2008, the Chairman of the Federal Reserve System asked Congress for authority to oversee systemically important payment and settlement systems, noting that many major central banks around the world have that explicit statutory authority.[58] In that testimony, Chairman Bernanke stated that "the stability of the broader financial system requires key payment and settlement systems to operate smoothly under stress and to effectively manage counterparty risk."[59]

Prior to the enactment of Title VIII, United States and international regulatory authorities called for the strengthening of the supervisory oversight of the financial infrastructure for payment and settlement systems. The U.S. Department of the Treasury issued reports during both the Bush and Obama Administrations recommending that oversight of systemically important payment and settlement systems should be given to the Federal Reserve.[60]

The Federal Reserve, together with other regulators and the private sector, was also engaged in efforts to strengthen various financial infrastructures prior to the Dodd-Frank Act. In 2005, the Federal Reserve Bank of New York began leading an initiative with industry participants to strengthen clearing and settling of credit default swaps and other OTC derivatives.[61] In addition, the Federal Reserve Bank of New York has worked with the private sector to enhance the oversight of tri-party repurchase agreements (repos[62]).[63]

Pre-Dodd-Frank Oversight

Prior to the Dodd-Frank Act, the Federal Reserve had prudential oversight responsibilities for key private-sector infrastructure systems, including CHIPS, CLS, DTCC (and its three primary subsidiaries, DTC, NSCC, and FICC), ICE Trust, and SWIFT.[64] The Federal Reserve had authority to oversee certain firms or their PCS activities under its statutory authority to conduct monetary policy and banking supervision, to act as the lender of last resort, and to supervise the Federal Reserve Banks' provision of payment and settlement services.[65] Other federal and state regulatory agencies also exercised prudential oversight of PCS systems and activities within their supervisory jurisdiction. For example, DTC was supervised by the New York State Banking Department based on its charter as a limited-purpose trust company under New York law. In addition, DTC was regulated by the Federal Reserve as a Fed member institution and by the SEC as a registered clearing agency.

The Federal Reserve also has supervisory authority (under the Federal Reserve Act) with respect to the Federal Reserve Banks' operation of key payment and settlement systems, including the Fedwire Funds Service and the Fedwire Securities Service. The Federal Reserve Board sets policy and is responsible for general supervision and oversight of the Federal Reserve Banks, including the provision of payment services.[66] Under such authority, the Federal Reserve conducts regular reviews of these systems and periodic assessments of the Fedwire Services against the relevant international standards. The prudential regulators include the CFTC for derivatives clearing organizations, the SEC for clearing agencies, and the federal bank regulatory agencies for depository institutions. Prior to the enactment of the Dodd-Frank Act, the SEC regulated clearing agencies (CAs) under the authority of the Exchange Act, sections 17, 17A and 19. CAs had to register with the SEC but were considered self-regulating organizations (SROs). Registration required compliance with established rules and a list of organizational and capacity standards. Because CAs are SROs though, little more was required of them other than filing to register with the SEC. Although they had to provide SEC any proposed changes to their rules, and self-enforce compliance to ensure that participants abided by these rules, CAs established the rules for their own industry.[67] While the SEC has maintained the authority to adopt rules for CAs deemed necessary and appropriate to the public interest, Dodd-Frank looks to codify more specifically enhanced risk management standards.

The CFTC, for its part, had regulatory authority over derivatives clearing organizations (DCO) under the Commodities Exchange Act (CEA). A DCO had to register with the CFTC and comply with 18 core principles in order to maintain its registration. The core principles ranged in topic from risk management to default rules to information sharing, among others. DCOs were granted authority to implement their own rules, but they had to comply with the CEA and be approved by the CFTC. While the CFTC program takes a "risk-based approach," Title VII and VIII state more explicitly how DCOs are to operate.[68]

Supervisory Policies

The Federal Reserve Policy on Payment System Risk (PSR Policy) addresses the risks that payment and settlement activity present to the financial system and the Federal Reserve Banks.[69] The PSR Policy sets out the Board's views, principles and minimum standards applicable to risk management for private-sector and Federal Reserve Bank payment and settlement systems.[70] In addition, the Federal Reserve's Regulation F requires insured depository institutions to establish policies and procedures to avoid excessive exposures to any other depository institutions, including those created through the clearing and settlement of payments.[71]

Bank supervision guidelines include the 2003 *Interagency Paper on Sound Practices to Strengthen the Resilience of the U.S. Financial System* adopted by the Federal Reserve, SEC and OCC to improve the resilience of the private-sector clearing and settlement infrastructure following the events of September 11, 2001.[72] The goal of the Interagency Paper was to ensure the smooth operation of the financial system in the event of a wide-scale disruption.

A 2008 interagency agreement among the Federal Reserve, the CFTC, and the SEC reflects the agencies' intent to cooperate and share information in carrying out their respective regulatory and supervisory responsibilities with regard to central counterparties for credit default swaps.[73]

The CFTC has also entered into an international interagency agreement with the United Kingdom Financial Services Authority (FSA) regarding derivatives clearing organizations and clearing houses based in the UK. In 2009, the CFTC and FSA signed a memorandum of understanding (MOU) that establishes a framework expressing their willingness to cooperate in the interest of fulfilling their statutory functions with respect to the clearing organizations, including on-site visits of respective clearing organizations.[74]

International Regulatory Standards

International banking regulators have also taken actions to identify risks related to PCS systems and to strengthen the financial infrastructure. The Committee for Payments and Settlement Systems (CPSS) was set up in 1990 under the aegis of the Bank for International Settlements (BIS) by the central banks of the Group of 10[75] countries. In 2009, the CPSS enlarged its membership to include many other important central banks. The CPSS meets three times annually and promotes sound and efficient payment and settlement systems. The CPSS acts as an international standard-setting body for payment and securities settlement systems and as a forum for central banks to monitor and analyze developments in domestic PCS systems and cross-border and multicurrency settlement systems.[76]

The standards consist of the Core Principles for Systemically Important Payment Systems (January 2001)[77] and two sets of recommendations published together with IOSCO (International Organization of Securities Commissions),[78] the Recommendations for Securities Settlement Systems (November 2001)[79] and the Recommendations for Central Counterparties (May 2004).[80] In February 2010, the CPSS and IOSCO launched a comprehensive review of the three sets of standards for financial market infrastructures with a view to strengthening them where appropriate.[81]

The CPSS also publishes policy reports analyzing issues related to large-value payment systems, retail payment instruments and systems, settlement mechanisms for foreign exchange transactions, and clearing and settlement of securities and derivatives transactions.[82] A CPSS report from May 2005 expressed the view that a core responsibility of central banks is the oversight function with respect to payment and settlement systems.[83]

In September 2010, the CPSS published a report entitled *Strengthening Repo Clearing and Settlement Arrangements* after the repo markets proved to be a less reliable source of funding liquidity than expected in some countries during the recent financial crisis.[84]

The CPSS published another report in April 2012 entitled *Principles for Financial Market Infrastructures, Assessment Methodology and Disclosure Framework.*[85] The report establishes international standards for payment, clearing and settlement systems, including central counterparties, that are more demanding than previous standards. The new set of standards replaces the previous set. The new standards raise minimum risk requirements, provide more specific guidance, and increase the number of institutions under its purview. Members of CPSS have been encouraged to adopt the new standards by the end of 2012.

TITLE VIII OF THE DODD-FRANK ACT

Title VIII of the *Dodd-Frank Wall Street Reform and Consumer Protection Act*, P.L. 111-203 establishes a regulatory framework for systemically important utilities and systemically important PCS activities conducted by financial institutions. It provides explicit statutory oversight authority to the Federal Reserve (Fed) in coordination with an entity's chartering and supervisory authority, establishing a consistent framework across supervisory authorities.

The Dodd-Frank Act also affects PCS systems and activities through Title VII, the *Wall Street Transparency and Accountability Act of 2010*, which establishes a comprehensive regulatory framework in regard to the over-the-counter (OTC) derivatives market and swap transactions.[86] Title VII establishes requirements for the clearing of certain bilateral swap transactions through derivatives clearinghouses.

Title VII also strengthens regulatory oversight of designated clearing entities (registered derivatives clearing organizations and clearing agencies) by the CFTC and the SEC, which are subject to the regulatory framework established in Title VIII.

The Senate, but not the House of Representatives, passed a version of the financial reform bill containing a title similar to Title VIII.[87] The House Financial Services Committee considered but struck by amendment a similar title in mark up, prior to the House of Representatives' floor consideration of the financial reform bill, H.R. 4173. Both the version of Title VIII in the Senate's bill and the version offered in the Conference Committee were modeled on proposed legislation released by the Obama Administration in 2009.[88]

During the Conference Committee, participants agreed to changes that enhanced the authority of the CFTC and SEC with respect to their supervised entities. The changes to the relevant title gave the CFTC and the SEC rule-writing authority for risk management standards and excluded some of their supervised entities from definitions and Federal Reserve oversight.

Title VIII defines *systemically important* and *systemic importance* apply to a situation where the failure of or a disruption to the functioning of a financial market utility or the conduct of a PCS activity could create or increase the risk of significant liquidity or credit problems spreading among financial institutions or markets and thereby threaten the stability of the financial system of the United States.

In general, Title VIII defines a *supervisory agency* as the federal agency that has primary jurisdiction over a designated financial market utility under federal banking, securities, or commodity futures laws and means the SEC with respect to a registered clearing agency, the CFTC with respect to a registered derivatives clearing organization, the appropriate federal banking agency with respect to an institution described in section 3(q) of the Federal Deposit Insurance Act, and the Federal Reserve Board with respect to any other type of designated financial market utility.

Exclusions

Title VIII broadly defines FMU systems and activities, but then explicitly excludes several specific systems and activities from its scope. Section 803 of Title VIII excludes from the FMU definition specified registered trading entities (exchanges) and data repositories registered and subject to CFTC oversight, including designated contract markets and swap data repositories, or registered and subject to SEC oversight, including national securities exchanges and swap execution facilities. Those exclusions are limited to the activities that require the entities to be registered.

Other exclusions from the FMU definition apply to various parties that act as intermediaries, including any broker, dealer, transfer agent, investment company, futures commission merchant, introducing broker, commodity trading advisor, or commodity pool operator. Such exclusions are limited to functions performed as part of the institution's named business. Also excluded are activities conducted by such institutions on behalf of a FMU or an FMU participant so long as the activities are not part of the FMU's critical risk management or processing functions.

Section 803 excludes from the financial institutions (FI) definition *designated clearing entities*, which are the systemically important DCOs and CAs subject to oversight by the CFTC and the SEC, respectively. The exclusion applies to the activities that require the entity to be registered. Thus, Title VIII regulation could apply to those entities only as FMUs rather than FIs.

Section 803 also excludes from the FI definition those registered trading entities (exchanges) and data repositories subject to CFTC or SEC oversight that are excluded from the definition of an FMU, such as designated contract markets, swap data repositories, and swap execution facilities, and additionally other entities, including securities information processors. The exclusion applies to the activities that require the entity to be registered.

FSOC Determines Systemic Importance

Congress provides a role to the newly created Financial Stability Oversight Council (Council) in the enhanced regulatory oversight framework in Title VIII. The members of the Council include the Secretary of the Treasury as Chairperson of the Council, the Chair of the Federal Reserve Board, and the heads of certain other agencies. The agencies with a role in

Title VIII (the CFTC, SEC, and the federal banking agencies) are all members of the Council.

Section 804 authorizes the Council to designate by at least a 2/3 vote, including the Chairperson (Secretary of the Treasury), those financial market utilities or PCS activities that the Council determines are, or are likely to become, systemically important. Prior to such determination, the Council shall consult with the relevant Supervisory Agency and the Federal Reserve Board.[89] The Council may similarly rescind a designation of systemic importance at any time.

The Council has broad authority to determine systemic importance. In addition to four listed factors, Congress provides that the Council shall consider any other factor that the Council deems appropriate. The Council must consider the following statutory factors:

- first, the aggregate monetary value of transactions processed by the utility or carried out through the PCS activity;
- second, the aggregate exposure of the utility or financial institution to its counterparties;
- third, the relationship, interdependencies, or other interactions of the utility or PCS activity with other financial market utilities or PCS activities; and,
- fourth, the effect that the failure of or a disruption to the utility or PCS activity would have on critical markets, financial institutions, or the broader financial system.

The Council must give advance notice of the proposed determination and opportunity for a written or oral hearing before the Council to the utility or financial institution.

The Council may waive or modify those procedural safeguards, however, upon 2/3 vote, including the Chairperson, if necessary to prevent or mitigate an immediate threat to the financial system posed by the utility or PCS activity.

The Council's final determination must be made within 60 days of any hearing or 30 days after the expiration of the opportunity to request a hearing, and the Council may extend the time periods affecting the consultation, notice, and hearing process.

In connection with assessing systemic importance, the Council may require any utility or financial institution to submit information as the Council may require if the Council has reasonable cause to believe that the utility or PCS activity meets the standards for systemic importance.[90]

Risk Management Standards

The statutory changes made by Title VIII are consistent with the view of international banking authorities that the oversight of payment and settlement systems is a core responsibility of central banks. Except with respect to designated clearing entities, section 805 of Title VIII authorizes the Fed to prescribe risk management standards, in consultation with the Council and Supervisory Agencies, governing the operations related to PCS activities of systemically important financial market utilities and the conduct of systemically important PCS activities by financial institutions. The Fed may prescribe such standards by rule or order and must take into consideration relevant international standards and existing prudential requirements.

The CFTC and the SEC may each prescribe regulations, in consultation with the Council and the Fed, containing risk management standards of similar scope for systemically important DCOs and CAs, respectively, and supervised financial institutions (for example, a futures commission merchant supervised by the CFTC) that engage in systemically important PCS activities. Those regulations, like the Fed's standards, must take into consideration relevant international standards and existing prudential requirements.

If the Fed determines that CFTC or SEC rules are insufficient to prevent or mitigate certain risks to the financial markets or to the financial stability of the United States, the Fed may impose risk management standards on an SEC- or CFTC-regulated entity. If the CFTC or the SEC objects within 60 days of the Fed's determination, then the Council would decide with a 2/3 vote which agency's risk management standards would apply.

The standards of the Fed, the CFTC, and the SEC may address areas such as risk management policies and procedures, margin and collateral requirements, participant or counterparty default policies and procedures, the ability to complete timely clearing and settlement of financial transactions, and capital and financial resource requirements for designated financial market utilities.[91] The agencies' standards must, where appropriate, establish a threshold of the amount (level or significance) of an institution's activity that will cause the standards to apply to the institution.

The Fed and the Council may not impose standards with respect to certain specified areas under CFTC or SEC authority, including the approval of clearing requirements, transaction reporting, or trade execution.[92] Further, pursuant to section 811, Title VIII in general does not divest any federal or state agency of any authority derived from any other applicable law. However, any standards prescribed by the Federal Reserve Board under section 805 shall supersede any less stringent requirements established under other authority.

Federal Reserve Services for Systemically Important Financial Market Utilities

Section 806 applies four Federal Reserve services or requirements to FMUs that apply to depository institutions. First, designated utilities may have certain accounts and deposit accounts at Federal Reserve Banks provided to depository institutions. Second, Federal Reserve Banks may pay earnings on balances maintained by a designated utility to the same extent paid to depository institutions. Third, the Fed may exempt a designated utility from reserve requirements or modify any applicable reserve requirement. Lastly, the Fed may authorize a Federal Reserve Bank to provide discount and borrowing privileges to a designated utility, but only in unusual or exigent circumstances and upon majority vote of the Fed after consultation with the Secretary of the Treasury. The utility would have to show that it is unable to secure adequate credit accommodations from other banking institutions.

Title VIII also establishes procedures that a systemically important financial market utility must follow when proposing changes to its rules, procedures, or operations. The designated utility must provide its Supervisory Agency with 60 days' advance notice of a proposed change that could materially affect the nature or level of risks presented by the utility. If the agency objects within 60 days, the utility may not implement the change. However, a designated utility may implement changes on an emergency basis in order for the utility to provide its services in a safe and sound manner.

Examination and Enforcement

Section 807 requires a Supervisory Agency to conduct examinations at least annually of a systemically important financial market utility to assess compliance with Title VIII.[93] In addition to standard-setting authority, Congress gives the Fed a role in examinations conducted by prudential regulators and enforcement for compliance with Title VIII. The Fed may, at its discretion, participate in an examination of a systemically important utility and may exercise back-up examination authority of a financial institution in certain circumstances. Title VIII also enables the Fed to take enforcement actions directly when necessary and with the Council's approval.

The Supervisory Agency must consult with the Fed at least annually regarding the scope of such examinations. The Fed in its discretion may participate in such examinations led by the Supervisory Agency. After consulting with the Council and Supervisory Agency, the Fed may at any time recommend that the agency take enforcement action to prevent risks to the financial markets or the financial stability of the United States. In the event of imminent risk of substantial harm to financial institutions, critical markets, or the U.S. financial system, the Fed with the affirmative vote of the Council may take enforcement action against the designated utility.

Section 808 authorizes the appropriate financial regulator of a financial institution to examine such institution with respect to a systemically important PCS activity for compliance with Title VIII. The Fed may consult with, and provide technical assistance to, the appropriate financial regulator, and the regulator may ask the Fed to conduct or participate in such examination or enforce Title VIII against the financial institution. Title VIII also gives the Fed back-up examination and enforcement authority, which the Fed may exercise with the Council's approval under certain conditions, including having reasonable cause to believe that a financial institution is not in compliance with Title VIII.

Title VIII extends certain enforcement provisions of section 8 of the Federal Deposit Insurance Act[94] to a systemically important financial market utility to the same extent as if the utility were an insured depository institution and to a financial institution subject to standards for a systemically important PCS activity.

Regulatory Coordination

As described in the purposes of Title VIII in Section 802, Congress is trying to mitigate systemic risk in the financial system and promote financial stability by authorizing the Board to promote uniform risk management standards for relevant institutions.

It also aims to accomplish this by providing the Board an enhanced role in the supervision of such standards. Title VIII, however, in general maintains certain regulatory and supervisory authority of the CFTC and SEC with respect to designated clearing entities. Further, Title VIII establishes various limitations requiring the Fed to consult with or act in coordination with the primary supervisor of a utility or financial institution and to obtain approval of the Council to exercise certain authority.

The Council similarly must consult with or act in coordination with other agencies in certain circumstances.

Title VIII does not remove prudential oversight by federal and state regulatory and supervisory agencies of their supervised institutions. In general, the Federal Reserve must exercise its new authority and responsibilities in coordination with prudential regulators. In some circumstances, however, the Federal Reserve may take actions, or seek approval of the Financial Stability Oversight Council to take actions, without the agreement of the primary supervisory agency.

The following provisions illustrate examples of required regulatory coordination under Title VIII:

- the Council must consult with the Fed and Supervisory Agencies in making systemic importance determinations under Section 804;
- the Fed or the Council must coordinate with a utility's Supervisory Agency or a financial institution's supervisor to request material information from or impose reporting or recordkeeping requirements on the entity under Section 809;
- the Fed, Council, Supervisory Agency, and appropriate financial regulator are authorized to promptly notify each other of material concerns about a designated utility or financial institution engaged in designated activities and share appropriate reports, information, or data relating to such concerns under Section 809(e); and
- coordination of examination and enforcement authority under Sections 807 and 808 is required, except to the extent that the Fed may exercise back-up or independent authority in limited circumstances.

Under Section 811, Title VIII does not divest agencies of existing authority derived from other applicable law except that standards prescribed by the Fed supersede any less stringent requirements established under other authority to the extent of a conflict.

The Conference Committee added certain provisions that limit the role of the Federal Reserve with respect to entities supervised by the CFTC and SEC. For example, Section 805 authorizes the CFTC and SEC to prescribe risk management standards for designated clearing entities (registered derivatives clearing organizations and registered clearing agencies), which the Fed can potentially override with the approval of the Council.

Title VIII also requires the CFTC and SEC to exercise certain authority in coordination with the Fed. Section 812 requires the CFTC and SEC to consult with the Fed prior to exercising authorities, including rulemaking authorities, under various provisions of law as amended by Title VIII. Section 813 requires the CFTC and the SEC to coordinate with the Fed to jointly develop risk management supervision programs for designated clearing entities.

TITLE VIII IMPLEMENTATION

Financial Stability Oversight Council

FSOC promulgated final rules for Title VIII on July 18, 2011. The rules authorized FSOC to designate financial market utilities it deemed systemically important. FSOC determines whether an FMU is systemically important if any failure of an FMUs operations could "create or increase the risk of significant liquidity or credit problems spreading among financial institutions or markets and thereby threaten the stability of the U.S. financial system."[95]

Federal Reserve

Section 805 of the Dodd-Frank Act provides that, except for certain entities supervised by the CFTC and SEC, the Federal Reserve by rule or order shall prescribe risk management standards governing operations of systemically important utilities and the conduct of systemically important activities by financial institutions.

On July 30, 2012, The Federal Reserve released its final rule regarding FMUs. It comprises much of the same material that was included in the proposed rules. The final rule implements risk management standards for FMUs, and standards for determining when FMUs must give notice about changes to rules, procedures, or operations that would alter the nature of risks they present.

The addition of two rules, one centering on application waivers, and the other revising the list of changes that do not require notice, mark the difference between the final rule and the proposed rule.[96]

CFTC and SEC

Title VIII provides the CFTC and the SEC, respectively, with additional authority to supervise and regulate those systemically important utilities that are derivatives clearing organizations (DCOs) and clearing agencies (CAs), which together are called designated clearing entities.

Section 805 of the Dodd-Frank Act authorizes the CFTC and SEC to prescribe regulations containing risk management standards governing the operations of designated clearing entities or the conduct of designated activities by financial institutions that each agency supervises.

Although the Fed may challenge such rules as insufficient, the CFTC and SEC may object to the Council regarding the Fed's determination. The Council would make the final decision upon the affirmative 2/3 vote of its members.

In July 2011, the Fed, CFTC, and SEC outlined the rulemaking governing their new authorities over DCOs and CAs, detailing the enhanced risk management standards these entities must follow.[97]

That rulemaking has since been largely finalized. For instance, the SEC announced final rules on June 28, 2012 specifying registering and review procedures for CAs.[98]

The CFTC announced a final rule on April 9, 2012, adopting new Dodd-Frank statutory provisions.[99]

The scope of Title VIII encompasses the infrastructure for the clearing of OTC derivatives, which is governed by the regulatory framework established in Title VII of the Dodd-Frank Act. Title VII requires firms to clear certain OTC derivatives, including credit default swaps, through central counterparties. Both the CFTC and the SEC must write various rules to implement Title VII, which will apply to derivatives clearing organizations and clearing agencies supervised by those agencies.[100] The clearing requirements in Title VII could increase the likelihood of a systemic importance designation under Title VIII for financial market utilities that engage in clearing OTC derivatives.

Impact on Payment, Clearing, and Settlement Systems and Activities

Those financial market utilities and PCS activities conducted by financial institutions that are designated as systemically important will be affected by additional supervision and requirements to comply with newly adopted risk management and conduct standards. Further, those designated firms could potentially be subject to increased oversight through the Federal Reserve's enhanced examination authority and role in enforcing compliance with applicable rules.

Certain payment system infrastructures were previously subject to Federal Reserve or other agency oversight.

Newer systems and technologies may be developed in the future to process financial transactions via the Internet and by other means. The impact on evolving technologies would depend upon the extent to which their activities fall within the scope of the supervisory framework established under the Dodd-Frank Act and whether newer systems become systemically important.

The impact of Title VIII on a particular entity is likely to vary depending upon whether a financial market utility or financial institution is currently subject to Federal Reserve supervision, whether a system or institution has operated previously outside the scope of bank regulatory or other federal agency oversight, and whether the utility or institution will also be subject to requirements and potentially increased clearing transaction volume under Title VII requirements.

The impact of Title VIII will also depend upon the actions of various regulators such as how broadly the Financial Stability Oversight Council applies the designation of systemic importance to financial market utilities and PCS activities of financial institutions and how stringently the Fed, CFTC and SEC decide to set risk management rules and standards.

List of Acronyms of Selected Terms

ACH	Automated clearing house
ANPR	Advance Notice of Proposed Rulemaking
BIS	Bank for International Settlements
CA	Clearing agency
CCP	Central counterparty
CDS	Credit default swap
CFTC	U.S. Commodity Futures Trading Commission
Council	Financial Stability Oversight Council
CPSS	Committee on Payment and Settlement Systems
DCO	Derivatives clearing organization

Appendix. Selected Payment, Clearing, and Settlement Systems in the United States

Table A-1. Selected FMUs Designated Systematically Important by FSOC

The Depository Trust Company	Central securities depository. DTC is a member of the Federal Reserve System, a limited-purpose trust company under New York State banking law supervised by the New York State Banking Department, and a registered clearing agency with the SEC.	The Depository Trust & Clearing Corporation (DTCC). DTCC is owned by its users, including major banks, broker-dealers, and other financial institutions.	Banks and broker-dealers. In 2008, there were 413 participants.	Settling trades in corporate, municipal, and mortgage-backed securities.	DTC moves securities for net settlements of the NSCC, which is also owned by DTCC, and settlement forinstitutional trades typically involving money and securities transfers between custodian banks and broker-dealers as well as money market instruments	In 2011, processed 302.3 million transactions, a 2.0% increase from 2010, valued at $1.669 quadrillion. The average value per transaction was $5.5 million.
National Securities Clearing Corporation (NSCC)	Regulated by the SEC	DTCC, which is owned by its users, including major banks, broker-dealers, and other financial institutions.	Brokers. In 2008, there were 221 participants.	Clearing, settlement, and central counterparty services for virtually all broker-to-broker trades in the U.S. involving equities and corporate and municipal debt.		In 2011, cleared 20.8 billion transactions, a 2.0% increase from 2010, valued at $220.9 trillion. The average value per transaction was $10.5 thousand.

Fixed Income Clearing Corporation (FICC)	Registered with and regulated by the SEC. Operates two divisions, the Government Securities Division (GSD) and the Mortgage-Backed Securities Division (MBSD). Each division offers services to their own members pursuant to separate rules and procedures.	DTCC, which is owned by its users, including major banks, broker-dealers, and other financial institutions.	GSD: broker-dealers, banks, and other financial institutions trading in the U.S. government-securities marketplace. In 2008, there were 97 participants in the GSD. MBSD: participants include mortgage originators, government-sponsored enterprises, broker-dealers, banks, and other financial institutions. In 2008, there were 103 participants in the MBSD.	GSD is a central counterparty and provides real-time trade matching, netting, and clearing services for trades in U.S. government debt issues, including repurchase (repo) agreements. MBSD provides real-time trade matching, netting, and clearing services for the mortgage-backed securities market.	Securities transactions processed by GSD include Treasury bills, bonds, notes, and government agency securities.	In 2011, GSD cleared 40.5 million transactions, a 19% increase from 2010, valued at $1.13 quadrillion. The average value per transaction was $27.9 million. In 2011, MBSD cleared 3.9 million transactions, a 22% increase from 2010, valued at $97.7 trillion. The average value per transaction was $25 million.
The Clearing House Payments Company	Payment, clearing and settlement operator. Operates CHIPS, EPN, and SVPCO Image. Regulated by the Federal Reserve.	Owned by Member banks and financial institutions. Member banks are among the largest banks in the world.	Provides payment, clearing, and settlement services to member banks and financial institutions.	Under CHIPS, provides payment, clearing, and settlement services in real time using U.S. dollars. Under EPN,operates private ACH services. And under SVPCO Image Exchange, provides settlement and reporting of digital images of paper checks.	Chips processes wire transfer payments for banks. EPN handles payroll, dividends, and other types of credit transfers. SVPCO Image, provides check images throughout a network of financial institutions.	The value of CHIPS transactions in 2011 amounte to $403.3 trillion. That same year, the average daily dollar amount exceeded $1.6 trillion. 52 banks participated with a total of 95 thousand transactions.

Table A-1. (Continued)

Chicago Mercantile Exchange The Options Clearing Corporation	Futures trading industry regulated by the Federal Reserve. Operates under the jurisdiction of both the CFTC (registered DCO) and the SEC.	Owned by theCME Group, which provides the largest options and futures products of any exchange in the world. CME Group is comprised of NYMEX, CBOT, COMEX, and CME. Founded in 1973, is the world's largest DCO. The stockholder exchanges share equal ownership of the OCC.	Traders and investors in options and futures contracts whc are members of the CME. Approximate y 130 of the largest U.S. broker-dealers, U.S. futures commission merchants, and non-U.S. securities firms representing professional traders and public customers.	An exchange that allows members to trade products and to trade directly on trading floor. Serves role as guarantor and central counterparty. Daily settlement of U.S. dollar payments is effected through a network of money-center banks	Principal transactions are trading various types of derivative products like futures and options. Under SEC jurisdiction, clears transactions for options and security futures. As DCO, provides clearing and settlement services for transactions in futures and options on futures.	In August 20 the average volume was 91 million for futures and 15 million for options. In 2011, processed 4.5 billion options contracts (daily average of 18.1 million) and 38.2 million futures contracts (daily average 151 thousand)
ICE Trust	Limited purpose New York trust company (New York State Banking Department). Member of the Federal Reserve System. Operates under an exemption from the SEC and the U.S. Treasury Department.	Operated by Intercontinental Exchange, a publicly listed company, which operates three regulated futures exchanges, trading platforms, clearinghouses, and over-the-counter markets.	14 clearing firm members. Customers of ICE are commercial hedgers, traders, brokers, risk managers, futures commission merchants, and portfolio managers.	Central credit facility for credit default swaps (CDS). Began clearing CDS contracts in March 2009.	Offers CDS clearing for 89 single-name and 38 index contracts.	Between March 2009 and August 2012, cleared approximately 267 thousand corporate and sovereign single-name CDS trades (with a gross notional cleared value of $1.835 trillion) and 240 thousand index CDS trades (with a gross notional cleared value of $17.4 trillion).

CLS Bank	Multi-currency cash settlement system founded in 1997	Financial services institutions in the foreign exchange business.	Settlement members and user members.	Settles payment instructions related to trades executed in six traded instruments and in 17 major currencies. Eliminates risk associated with foreign exchange settlement across time zones.	Foreign exchange	Settles 55% of the world's foreign exchange payment instructions (as of August 2012,)

Source: CPSS Publication No 88, Red Book Statistical Update, Statistics on payment and settlement systems in selected countries, December 2009, available at http://www.bis.org/publ/cpss88.htm; U.S. Department of the Treasury, Blueprint for a Modernized Financial Regulatory Structure, March 2008; Federal Reserve website at http://www.federalreserve.gov/paymentsystems/ fedfunds_data.htm, and http://www.federalreserve.gov/ paymentsystems/fedsecs_ data.htm; Volume/Value data acquired from websites of selected systems each accessed in August 2012.Click here and type the source, or delete this paragraph.

Table A-2. Other PCS Systems

Name	Type/Regulator	Owners/Operators	Users/Participants	Uses/Functions	Transactions	Volume/Value
Fedwire Funds Service	Real-time gross settlement system (RGSS). Payments are continuously settled on an individual, order-by-order basis without netting. Transfer of funds is final and irrevocable when settled.	Federal Reserve/Federal Reserve Banks	Depository institutions, U.S. Treasury, Federal government agencies. In 2008, there were 5,458 participants (excluding the U.S. Treasury and certain other domestic and foreign entities), a decrease from the 6,388 participants in 2007.	Sending funds to other institutions, including for customers. Payment orders by depository institutions are processed individually and settled in central bank money upon receipt. The U.S. Treasury and other	Purchase and sale of federal funds (depository institutions lend balances at the Federal Reserve to other depository institutions overnight); purchase, sale, and financing of securities	In 2011, there were 127 million transfers originated (a 1.5% increase from 2010), valued at $663 trillion. The average value per transfer was $5.23 million. In 2012 (Q1), the average daily volume of transfers

Table A-2. (Continued)

Name	Type/Regulator	Owners/Operators	Users/Participants	Uses/Functions	Transactions	Volume/Value
				federal agencies use this service to disburse and receive funds.	transactions; disbursement or repayment of loans; settlement of cross-border U.S. dollar commercial transactions; settlement of real estate transactions and other high-value, time-critical payments.	(for business days) was 514 thousand with an average daily value of $2.35 trillion.
Fedwire Securities Service (National Book-Entry System)	Real-time transfers on individual or gross basis. Transfer of securities and related funds, if any, is final and irrevocable when made. Most securities transfers involve the simultaneous exchange of payment known as delivery versus payment (DVP), which ensures that the final transfer of securities	Federal Reserve/Federal Reserve Banks. The Federal Reserve Banks act as fiscal agents to facilitate the issuance of book-entry securities to participants.	Limited to depository institutions and a few other entities, including the U.S. Treasury, government-sponsored enterprises, state treasurers, and limited-purpose trust companies that are members of the Federal Reserve System. Nonbank broker-dealers typically hold and transfer their Fedwire securities through depository institution participants. In 2008, there were 1,203	Issuance, transfer, and settlement for all marketable Treasury securities, for many federal government agency and government-sponsored enterprise securities, and for certain international organizations' securities. There is a safekeeping function (electronic storage of securities holding records in custody accounts) and a	Transfer of securities – for example, to settle secondary market trades, including open market operations; to move collateral used to secure obligations; and to facilitate repurchase (repo) agreement transactions.	In 2011, there were 18.6 million transfers originated (a 5.9% decrease from 2010), valued at $291.8 trillion. The average value per transfer was $15.6 million. In 2012 (Q1), the average daily volume of transfers (for business days) was 74.6 thousand with an average daily value of $1.1 trillion. Securities

Name	Type/Regulator	Owners/Operators	Users/Participants	Uses/Functions	Transactions	Volume/Value
	occurs if and only if the final transfer of payment occurs.		participants in NBES.	transfer and settlement function (electronic transfer of securities between parties with or without a settlement payment).		held in custody at end of 2nd quarter 2010 were $61 trillion.
National Settlement Service (NSS)	Multilateral settlement service implemented in March 1999. Settlement finality occurs on day of settlement.	Federal Reserve/ Federal Reserve Banks	Depository institutions that settle for participants in clearinghouses, financial exchanges, and other clearing and settlement groups. Key private-sector system users include DTC and NSCC for end-of-day cash settlement; FICC for funds-only settlement; EPN; The Options Clearing Corp; and several large and regional check clearinghouses.	Settlement agents acting on behalf of depository institution participants in a settlement arrangement electronically submit settlement files to the Federal Reserve Banks. The files are processed upon receipt, and entries are automatically posted to a depository institution's Federal Reserve account.	Currently, there are approximately 40 NSS arrangements establishes by financial market utilities, check clearinghouse associations, and automated clearinghouse networks.	In 2011, processed about 571,000 transfers valued at about $15.7 trillion. In 2012 (Q1), the average daily volume of entries processed was 2,585 with an average daily settlement value of $63.75 billion.
FedACH Service	Electronic payment system providing automated clearing house (ACH) services.	Federal Reserve/Federal Reserve Banks	Depository institutions	The ACH system exchanges batched debit and credit payments among business, consumer, and government accounts.	Pre-authorized recurring payments such as payroll, Social Security, mortgage, and utility payments. Non-recurring.	In 2009, originated 13.4 billion transactions with a value of $22.3 trillion.

Table A-2. (Continued)

Name	Type/Regulator	Owners/Operators	Users/Participants	Uses/Functions	Transactions	Volume/Value
					payments such as telephone-initiated payments and the conversion of checks into ACH payments at lockboxes and points of sale. Also outbound cross-border ACH payments through FedGlobal service	
Electronic Payments Network (EPN)	ACH operator	The Clearing House, which is owned by the largest U.S. banks or the U.S. branches or affiliates of major foreign banks.	Over 1350 financial institutions. Approximately 53% of customers are credit unions, 36% commercial, 9% savings, and 2% savings and loan institutions.	Payment system handling credit transfers such as payroll and dividends and debit transfers such as loan and bill payments and insurance premiums.	Processes 48% of all commercial ACH volume in the U.S.	Processes over 6.5 billion transactions annually.
Society for Worldwide Interbank Financial Telecommunication (SWIFT)	Financial messaging service	User-owned, limited liability cooperative organized under Belgian law headquartered in Belgium with operational centers in	More than 9,000 banking organizations, securities institutions, and corporate customers in 209 countries. U.S. financial intermediaries are among the heaviest	Provides secure, standardized financial messages and related services to its member financial institutions, their market		As of June 2012, processed 2.3 billion messages year-to-date, averaging 18.2 million messages per business day.

Name	Type/Regulator	Owners/Operators	Users/Participants	Uses/Functions	Transactions	Volume/Value
		the Netherlands and the United States.	users of SWIFT services for correspondent banking communications.	infrastructures, and their end-users.		

Dodd-Frank Act	Dodd-Frank Wall Street Reform and Consumer Protection Act
EFT	Electronic funds transfer
FFIEC	Federal Financial Institutions Examination Council
Fed	Federal Reserve System
FI	Financial institution
FMU	Financial market utility
FSA	United Kingdom Financial Services Authority
IOSCO	International Organization of Securities Commissions
MOU	Memorandum of Understanding
OTC	Over-the-counter
PCS	Payment, clearing, and settlement
PSR Policy	Federal Reserve Policy on Payment System Risk
Repo	Repurchase agreement
RTGS	Real-time gross settlement
SEC	U.S. Securities and Exchange Commission
Title VII	Wall Street Transparency and Accountability Act of 2010
Title VIII	Payment, Clearing, and Settlement Supervision Act of 2010

End Notes

[1] P.L. 111-203, the Dodd-Frank Wall Street Reform and Consumer Protection Act.

[2] See Federal Reserve Fedwire Funds Services website at http://www.federalreserve.gov/paymentsystems/fedfunds_ann.htm, and CHIPS annual statistics at http://www.chips.org/about/pages/001221.php. 2011 figures from Fedwire and CHIPS were added together.

[3] U.S. Department of the Treasury, Blueprint for a Modernized Financial Regulatory Structure, Washington, DC, March 2008, p. 102. AIG was also exposed to significant losses from its securities lending operation.

[4] John Glover and Hamish Risk, "Exchange-Traded Credit Derivatives Poised to Curb Bank Monopoly," Bloomberg, December 11, 2006.

[5] Bank for International Settlements, Committee on Payment and Settlement Systems, Central Bank Oversight of Payment and Settlement Systems, CPSS Publications No. 68, Basel, Switzerland, May 2005, p. 13, http://www.bis.org/ publ/cpss68.pdf. Hereinafter cited as BIS, Central Bank Oversight.

[6] Board of Governors of the Federal Reserve System, Financial Market Utilties, RIN No. 7100-AD 71, July 30, 2012, http://www.federalreserve.gov/newsevents/ press/bcreg/bcreg 20120730a1.pdf.

[7] See CRS Report R41398, The Dodd-Frank Wall Street Reform and Consumer Protection Act: Title VII, Derivatives, by Mark Jickling and Kathleen Ann Ruane.

[8] The Electronic Payments Network and other subsidiaries are deemed systemically important by default for being component parts of the parent company The Clearing House Payments Company, which was designated systemically important.

[9] U.S. Department of the Treasury, Blueprint for a Modernized Financial Regulatory Structure, Washington, DC, March 2008, p. 211.

[10] Federal Reserve Bank of New York, Fedwire and National Settlement Services, New York, New York. http://www.newyorkfed.org/aboutthefed/fedpoint/fed43.html.

[11] The relevant law is the Depository Institutions Deregulation and Monetary Control Act of 1980, P.L. 96-221, enacted on March 31, 1980.

[12] Federal Reserve Bank of New York, Fedwire and National Settlement Services, New York, New York, http://www.newyorkfed.org/aboutthefed/fedpoint/fed43.html.

[13] Board of Governors of the Federal Reserve System, Open Market Operations, Washington, DC, January 26, 2010, http://www.federalreserve.gov/monetarypolicy/openmarket.htm.

[14] Federal Reserve, Press Release, July 19, 2012, available at http://www.federalreserve.gov/ newsevents/press/bcreg/ 20120719a.htm.

[15] Bank for International Settlements, Committee for Payment and Settlement Systems, A Glossary of Terms Used in Payments and Settlement Systems, Basel, Switzerland, March 2003, http://www.bis.org/publ/cpss00b.pdf. Hereinafter cited as BIS, Glossary.

[16] For background information on retail and wholesale payment systems, see Federal Financial Institutions Examination Council, Retail Payment Systems, IT Examination Handbook, Washington, DC, February 2010, http://www.ffiec.gov/ ffiecinfobase/booklets/ Retail/retail.pdf, hereinafter cited as FFIEC, Retail Handbook; and Federal Financial Institutions Examination Council, Wholesale Payment Systems, IT Examination Handbook, Washington, DC, July 2004, http://www.ffiec.gov/ffiecinfobase/ booklets/Wholesale/whole. pdf, hereinafter cited as FFIEC, Wholesale Handbook.

[17] FFIEC, Retail Handbook, p. 4. Retail payment instruments include check-based payments, card-based and other electronic payments such as electronic cash and electronic benefits transfer, and ACH transactions.

[18] See Financial Management Service website, http://www.fms.treas.gov/ach/index.html.

[19] See Electronic Payments Network website, http://www.epaynetwork.com/cms/services/ 001456.php.

[20] The trade association was formerly known as the National Automated Clearing House Association.

[21] ACH transfers between financial institutions are not considered check transactions, and thus are not subject to laws governing check processing. FFIEC, Retail Handbook, p. 10.

[22] NACHA—The Electronic Payments Association, ACH Network Statistics, Herndon, VA, 2010, http://www.nacha.org/c/ACHntwkstats.cfm, visited August 31, 2012.

[23] FFIEC, Wholesale Handbook, p. 3.

[24] Fedwire participants maintain a reserve or securities account with a Federal Reserve Bank. Direct access to Federal Reserve payment services is generally limited to deposit-taking institutions; however, non-depository institutions may indirectly use those services as customers of Federal Reserve payment services participants. Ibid, p.4.

[25] CHIPS is operated by The Clearing House, which also operates the Electronic Payments Network, a private-sector provider of ACH services. CHIPS' website is http://www.chips.org/home.php.

[26] The Committee on Payment and Settlement Services defines netting as an agreed offsetting of positions or obligations by trading partners or participants. Netting reduces a large number of individual positions or obligations to a smaller number and may take several forms that have varying degrees of legal enforceability in the event of default of one of the parties. BIS, Glossary.

[27] U.S. Securities and Exchange Commission, Clearing Agencies, Washington, DC, http://www.sec.gov/divisions/ marketreg/mrclearing.shtml.

[28] Ibid.

[29] Ibid.

[30] The Depository Trust & Clearing Corporation, About DTCC, Our Structure, New York, New York, http://www.dtcc.com/about/subs/.

[31] U.S. Commodity Futures Trading Commission, Clearing Organizations, Derivatives Clearing Organizations, Washington, DC, http://www.cftc.gov/IndustryOversight/ ClearingOrganizations/index.htm.

[32] http://sirt.cftc.gov/SIRT/SIRT.aspx?Topic=ClearingOrganizations&implicit= true&type= DCO& CustomColumnDisplay=TTTTTTTT.

[33] Federal Financial Institutions Examination Council, Wholesale Payment Systems, IT Examination Handbook Presentations, Washington, DC, July 2004, p. 3, http://www.ffiec.gov/ffiecinfobase/presentations/ whole_presntation.pdf.

[34] FFIEC, Wholesale Handbook, p. 11.

[35] Ibid.

[36] Ibid. The Federal Reserve Banks in their capacity as fiscal agents facilitate the issuance of book-entry securities to the Fedwire Securities Service participants. The Fedwire Securities system maintains in electronic form all marketable U.S. Treasury securities as well as many federal government agency, GSE, and certain international organizations' securities. See Federal Reserve Bank Services, Fedwire Securities Service, http://www.frbservices.org /serviceofferings/ fedwire/fedwire_security_service.html.

[37] Commercial paper is a money market instrument issued by prime-rated non-financial and financial companies with maturities ranging from one to 270 days. Commercial paper is issued through dealer placements or direct placements with investors. Commercial paper is an important source of short-term funding for financial corporations and municipal governments and secondary market trading is limited. FFIEC, Wholesale Handbook, p. 14.

[38] The Depository Trust & Clearing Corporation, About DTCC, National Securities Clearing Corporation (NSCC), New York, New York, http://www.dtcc.com/about/subs/nscc.php.

[39] U.S. Department of the Treasury, Blueprint for a Modernized Financial Regulatory Structure, Washington, DC, March 2008, p. 101; U.S. Department of the Treasury, Financial Regulatory Reform, A New Foundation: Rebuilding Financial Supervision and Regulation, Washington, DC, June 2009, p. 52, http://www.financialstability.gov/docs/regs/ FinalReport_web.pdf. Hereinafter cited as 2009 New Foundation.

[40] James B. Thomson, On Systemically Important Financial Institutions and Progressive Systemic Mitigation, Federal Reserve Bank of Cleveland, Policy Discussion Paper Number 27, August 2009, p. 1, http://www.clevelandfed.org/ research/policydis/pdp27.pdf.

[41] International Monetary Fund, Meeting New Challenges to Stability and Building a Safer System, Global Financial Stability Report, April 2010, p. 2, http://www.imf. org/external/ pubs/ft/gfsr/2010/01/index.htm.

[42] For a discussion of provisions addressing systemic risk, see CRS Report R41384, The Dodd-Frank Wall Street Reform and Consumer Protection Act: Systemic Risk and the Federal Reserve, by Marc Labonte.

[43] Bank for International Settlements, Committee on Payment and Settlement Systems, The Interdependencies of Payment and Settlement Systems, CPSS Publications No. 84, Basel, Switzerland, June 2008, p. iii, http://www.bis.org/ publ/cpss84.pdf.

[44] Ibid., p. 27.

[45] Ibid.

[46] Ibid., p. 14.

[47] Bank for International Settlements, "Standards for Payment, Clearing, and Settlement Systems: Review by CPSSIOSCO," Basel, Switzerland, press release, February 2, 2010, http://www.bis.org/press/p100202.htm. Hereinafter cited as BIS, Standards Review Press Release.

[48] Ibid.

[49] See, e.g., Elena Logutenkova and Fabio Benedetti-Valentini, "Blankfein Says Clearinghouses May Increase Risks in Crisis," Bloomberg Businessweek, September 29, 2010, http://www. businessweek.com/news/2010-09-29/blankfeinsays-clearinghouses-may-increase-risks-in-crisis.html.

[50] Darrell Duffie and Haoxiang Zhu, "Does a Central Clearing Counterparty Reduce Counterparty Risk?," Graduate School of Business, Stanford University, Updated March 6, 2010, p. http://www.stanford.edu/~duffie/DuffieZhu.pdf.

[51] Section 802(a)(2) of the Dodd-Frank Act, P.L. 111-203.

[52] Board of Governors of the Federal Reserve System, Policy on Payment System Risk, Washington, DC, as amended effective June 16, 2010, http://federalreserve.gov/ paymentsystems/psr_policy.htm.

[53] See FFIEC, Wholesale Handbook, p. 21.

[54] Ibid., p. 27.

[55] Ibid., p. 18.

[56] See the discussion of prudential regulators in the next section of this report.

[57] Statement of Ben S. Bernanke, Chairman, Board of Governors of the Federal Reserve System, in U.S. Congress, House Committee on Financial Services, Systemic Risk and the Financial Markets, 110th Cong., 2nd sess., July 10, 2008, H.Hrg., p. 65 (Washington: GPO, 2008).

[58] Ibid.

[59] Ibid.

[60] U.S. Department of the Treasury, Blueprint for a Modernized Financial Regulatory Structure, Washington, DC, March 2008; 2009 New Foundation.

[61] Federal Reserve Bank of New York, "Statement Regarding Meeting on Credit Derivatives," press release, New York, New York, September 15, 2005, http://www.newyorkfed.org/ newsevents/news_archive/markets/2005/ an050915.html. For information on developments from this initiative, see Federal Reserve Bank of New York, OTC Derivatives Market Infrastructure, New York, New York, http://www.newyorkfed.org/ newsevents/ otc_derivative.html.

[62] A repo transaction is an agreement between two parties on the sale and subsequent repurchase of securities at an agreed price. In economic terms, a repo transaction is equivalent to a loan backed by collateral consisting of the securities. Bank for International Settlements, Committee on Payment and Settlement Systems, Strengthening Repo Clearing and Settlement Arrangements, CPSS Publications No. 91, Basel, Switzerland, September 2010, p. 5, http://www.bis.org/publ/cpss91.pdf. Hereinafter cited as BIS, Strengthening Repo.

[63] The Payments Risk Committee is a private sector group representing various U.S. banks. The Payments Risk Committee is sponsored by the Federal Reserve Bank of New York. See Federal Reserve Bank of New York, Payments Risk Committee, New York, New York,

http://www.newyorkfed.org/prc/. In May 2010, the Federal Reserve Bank of New York released a white paper on Tri-Party Repurchase Agreement (Repo) Reform. Federal Reserve Bank of New York, Tri-Party Repo Infrastructure Reform, White Paper, New York, New York, May 17, 2010, http://www.newyorkfed.org/banking/nyfrb_triparty_whitepaper.pdf.

[64] See Board of Governors of the Federal Reserve System, Oversight of Key Financial Market Infrastructures, Private-Sector Systems, Washington, DC, http://www.federalreserve.gov/paymentsystems/over_pssystems.htm.

[65] BIS, Central Bank Oversight, p. 13.

[66] Board of Governors of the Federal Reserve System, Oversight of Key Financial Market Infrastructures, Reserve Bank Systems, Washington, DC, http://www.federalreserve.gov/paymentsystems/over_rbsystems.htm.

[67] Board of Governors of the Federal Reserve, Securities and Exchange Commission, and Commodity Futures Trading Commission, Risk Management Supervision of Designated Clearing Entities, Securities and Exchange Commission, Washington, DC, July 1, 2011, pp. 19-22, http://www.sec.gov/news/studies/2011/813study.pdf.

[68] Board of Governors of the Federal Reserve, Securities and Exchange Commission, and Commodity Futurees Trading Commission, Risk Management Supervision of Desginated Clearing Entities, Securities and Exchange Commission, Washington, DC, July 2011, pp. 22-24, http://www.sec.gov/news/studies/2011/813study.pdf.

[69] The current PSR Policy, as amended effective June 16, 2010, is effective through March 23, 2011 and is accessible at http://www.federalreserve.gov/paymentsystems/psr_policy.htm. The PSR Policy that will become effective on March 24, 2011 is accessible at http://www.federalreserve.gov/paymentsystems/2011_psr_policy.htm.

[70] The PSR Policy also governs the provision of intraday or "daylight" credit provided by Federal Reserve Banks, including policies regarding overdrafts in accounts at Federal Reserve Banks, net debit caps, and daylight overdraft fees.

[71] 12 C.F.R. Part 206.

[72] Dated April 7, 2003. Issued with Board of Governors of the Federal Reserve System, Federal Reserve Supervisory Letter SR 03-9, Washington, DC, May 28, 2003, http://www.federalreserve.gov/boarddocs/srletters/2003/sr0309.htm.

[73] U.S. Department of the Treasury, "Memorandum of Understanding Between the Board, the CFTC, and the SEC Regarding Central Counterparties for Credit Default Swaps," press release, Washington, DC, November 14, 2008, http://www.ustreas.gov/press/releases/hp1272.htm.

[74] U.S. Commodity Futures Trading Commission, Memorandum of Understanding Concerning Cooperation and the Exchange of Information Related to the Supervision of Cross-Border Clearing Organizations, Washington, DC, September 14, 2009, http://www.cftc.gov/ucm/groups/public/@internationalaffairs/documents/file/ukfsa09.pdf.

[75] The Group of 10 or G10 includes the United States, the United Kingdom, Germany, France, Canada, Japan, Sweden, Italy, Switzerland, the Netherlands and Belgium (11 countries).

[76] Bank for International Settlements, Committee on Payment and Settlement Systems, CPSS Publications, Basel, Switzerland, http://www.bis.org/cpss/index.htm. The current chairman of the CPSS is William C. Dudley, President of the Federal Reserve Bank of New York. Timothy Geithner, then-President and Chief Executive Officer of the Federal Reserve Bank of New York, chaired the CPSS from 2005 to 2009. See Bank for International Settlements, CPSS History, Organisation, Cooperation, Basel, Switzerland, http://www.bis.org/cpss/cpssinfo01.htm.

[77] Bank for International Settlements, Committee on Payment and Settlement Systems, CPSS Publications No. 43, Basel, Switzerland, http://www.bis.org/publ/cpss43.pdf.

[78] IOSCO is a policy forum for securities regulators whose membership regulates more than 95% of the world's securities markets in over 100 jurisdictions.

[79] Bank for International Settlements, Committee on Payment and Settlement Systems, CPSS Publications No. 46, Basel, Switzerland, http://www.bis.org/publ/cpss46.pdf.

[80] Bank for International Settlements, Committee on Payment and Settlement Systems, CPSS Publications No. 64, Basel, Switzerland, http://www.bis.org/publ/cpss64.pdf.

[81] BIS, Standards Review Press Release. The CPSS expects to issue draft revised standards by early 2011. The International Monetary Fund and the World Bank are also participating in the CPSS-IOSCO standards review, which is part of the Financial Stability Board's work to reduce the risks that arise from interconnectedness in the financial system.

[82] See Bank for International Settlements, Committee on Payment and Settlement Systems, CPSS Publications, http://www.bis.org/cpss/index.htm.

[83] BIS, Central Bank Oversight, p. iii.

[84] BIS, Strengthening Repo.

[85] Committee on Payment and Settlement Systems, Principles for Financial Market Infrastructures, Bank for International Settlements, Basel, Switzerland, April 1, 2012, http://www.bis.org/publ/cpss101a.pdf.

[86] See CRS Report R41398, The Dodd-Frank Wall Street Reform and Consumer Protection Act: Title VII, Derivatives, by Mark Jickling and Kathleen Ann Ruane.

[87] S. 3217 contained the language of the Senate version of the financial reform bill. The Senate passed H.R. 4173, with an amendment in the nature of a substitute, replacing the House language with the text of S. 3217.

[88] U.S. Department of the Treasury, Title VIII, Washington, DC, http://www.financialstability.gov/docs/ regulatoryreform/title-VIII_payments_072209.pdf. For information on all of the proposed titles, see U.S. Department of the Treasury, http://www.financialstability.gov/roadtostability/timeline.html.

[89] By referring to the defined term "Supervisory Agency," this provision apparently does not require the Council to consult with a Federal banking regulator with respect to a financial institution that conducts a PCS activity but that is not a utility regardless of whether the PCS activity is determined to be systemically important.

[90] Because Title VIII does not set forth standards for systemic importance, this text apparently refers to statutory considerations rather than standards.

[91] Congress did not authorize regulators under Title VIII to modify existing prudential capital and financial resource requirements that apply to financial institutions conducting systemically important PCS activities.

[92] The Fed's enforcement authority under Section 807(e) and (f), however, is not subject to the same limitations.

[93] A Supervisory Agency also may examine services integral to the operation of the utility by a third-party service provider.

[94] 12 U.S.C. Section 1818(i).

[95] Financial Stability Oversight Council, "Final Rules," press release, January 18, 2011, available at http://www.treasury.gov/initiatives/fsoc/Pages/final-rules.aspx.

[96] Board of Governors of the Federal Reserve System, Financial Market Utilities, RIN No. 7100-AD 71, July 30, 2012, available at http://www.theclearinghouse.org/index.html?f=074147.

[97] Board of Governors of the Federal Reserve, Securities and Exchange Commission, and Commodity Futures Trading Commission, Risk Management Supervision of Designated

Clearing Entities, Securities and Exchange Commission, Washington, D.C., July 2011, p. 3, available at http://www.sec.gov/news/studies/2011/813study.pdf.

[98] Available at http://www.sec.gov/rules/final/2012/34-67286.pdf.

[99] Available at http://www.cftc.gov/ucm/groups/public/@lrfederalregister/documents/file/2012-7477a.pdf.

[100] International standards applicable to clearing organizations have also undergone revision. See, Committee on Payment and Settlement Systems, Principles for Financial Market Infrastructures, Bank for International Settlements, Basel, Switzerland, April 1, 2012, http://www.bis.org/publ/cpss101a.pdf. In May 2010, the CPSS and IOSCO released guidance with respect to how the 2004 Recommendations for central counterparties should be applied to the handling of OTC derivatives by central counterparties. Bank for International Settlements, Committee on Payment and Settlement Systems, Guidance on the Application of the 2004 CPSS-IOSCO Recommendations for Central Counterparties to OTC Derivatives CCPs – Consultative Report, CPSS Publications No. 89, Basel, Switzerland, May 2010, http://www.bis.org/publ/cpss89.pdf. In November 2010, the CPSS released a report entitled, Market Structure Developments in the Clearing Industry: Implications for Financial Stability. Bank for International Settlements, Committee on Payment and Settlement Systems, CPSS Publications No. 92, Basel, Switzerland, http://www.bis.org/publ/cpss92.pdf.

In: Financial Market Utilities ...
Editor: Jovan Barank
ISBN: 978-1-62618-052-9

Chapter 2

FINANCIAL MARKET UTILITIES: A RULE BY THE FEDERAL RESERVE SYSTEM*

Board of Governors of the Federal Reserve System

SUMMARY

The Board is publishing a final rule, Regulation HH, Designated Financial Market Utilities. This rule implements provisions of sections 805(a) and 806(e) of the Dodd-Frank Wall Street Reform and Consumer Protection Act ("Dodd-Frank Act" or "Act"), including risk-management standards for financial market utilities ("FMUs") that are designated as systemically important by the Financial Stability Oversight Council (the "Council") and standards for determining when a designated FMU is required to provide advance notice of proposed changes to its rules, procedures, or operations that could materially affect the nature or level of risks presented by the designated FMU.

DATES

This final rule is effective September 14, 2012.

* This is an edited, reformatted and augmented version of a Board of Governors of the Federal Reserve System publication, Document Citation: 77 FR 45907, dated 08/02/12.

I. BACKGROUND

Title VIII of the Dodd-Frank Act, titled the "Payment, Clearing, and Settlement Supervision Act of 2010," was enacted to mitigate systemic risk in the financial system and to promote financial stability, in part, through enhanced supervision of designated FMUs.[1] Section 803 of the Dodd-Frank Act defines an FMU as a person that manages or operates a multilateral system for the purpose of transferring, clearing, or settling payments, securities, or other financial transactions among financial institutions or between financial institutions and the person. The basic risks that FMUs must manage include credit risk, liquidity risk, settlement risk, operational risk, and legal risk. These risks arise between financial institutions and FMUs as they settle payments and other financial transactions. In order to maintain financial stability, FMUs must be well-designed and operated in a safe and sound manner. If a systemically important FMU fails to measure, monitor, and manage its risks effectively, it could pose significant risk to its participants and the financial system more broadly.

Under section 805(a)(1) of the Dodd-Frank Act, the Board is required to promulgate risk-management standards governing the operations related to the payment, clearing, and settlement ("PCS") activities of certain FMUs that are designated as systemically important by the Council. Section 805(a)(1) of the Act also requires the Board to take into consideration relevant international standards and existing prudential requirements in prescribing the regulations. For a designated FMU that is a derivatives clearing organization ("DCO") registered under section 5b of the Commodity Exchange Act or a clearing agency registered under section 17A of the Securities Exchange Act of 1934 (collectively, "designated clearing entities"), the Commodity Futures Trading Commission ("CFTC") or the Securities and Exchange Commission ("SEC"), respectively, are granted authority to prescribe regulations, in consultation with the Council and the Board, containing applicable risk-management standards.[2]

Section 805(b) of the Act sets out the following objectives and principles for the risk-management standards: (a) Promote robust risk management, (b) promote safety and soundness, (c) reduce systemic risks, and (d) support the stability of the broader financial system. Section 805(c) of the Act states that risk-management standards may address areas such as (1) risk-management policies and procedures, (2) margin and collateral requirements, (3) participant or counterparty default policies and procedures, (4) the ability to complete timely clearing and settlement of financial transactions, (5) capital and financial resource requirements for designated FMUs, and (6) other areas that are necessary to achieve the objectives and principles for risk-management standards.

In addition, section 806(e)(1) of the Dodd-Frank Act requires a designated FMU to provide 60 days' advance notice to its Supervisory Agency of any proposed change to its rules, procedures, or operations that could, as defined in rules of each Supervisory Agency, materially affect the nature or level of risks presented by the designated FMU. Under section 803(b) of the Act, a "Supervisory Agency" means the federal agency that has primary jurisdiction over a designated FMU under federal banking, securities, or commodity futures laws. [3]

In April 2011, the Board published for comment a notice of proposed rulemaking ("NPRM") to propose a new part to the Code of Federal Regulations (12 CFR part 234, Regulation HH) to establish risk-management standards for designated FMUs and requirements for advance notice of material changes to a designated FMU's rules, procedures, or operations. [4] The public comment period closed on May 19, 2011.

II. Summary of Public Comments and Analysis

The Board received twelve public comment letters on the NPRM. Comments were submitted by two payment systems, seven industry and other groups, one bank, and two other commenters. In general, the comments pertained broadly to three categories: (i) Risk-management standards, (ii) advance notice requirements and the materiality definition, and (iii) other miscellaneous comments. The Board considered these comments in developing its final rule as discussed in more detail below. [5]

A. Risk-Management Standards

1. International Standards

Proposed § 234.3 sets out risk-management standards for designated FMUs that are payment systems, and proposed § 234.4 sets out risk-management standards for central counterparties ("CCPs") and central securities depositories ("CSDs"), based on the international risk-management standards developed by the Committee on Payment and Settlement Systems ("CPSS") and the Technical Committee of the International Organization of

Securities Commissions ("IOSCO"). These international standards were the Core Principles for Systemically Important Payment Systems (the "Core Principles") developed by the CPSS in 2001, and the Recommendations for Securities Settlement Systems and the Recommendations for Central Counterparties (collectively, the "CPSS-IOSCO Recommendations") developed jointly by the CPSS and IOSCO in 2001 and 2004, respectively. The Board believes these standards are the appropriate basis for setting initial risk-management standards under Title VIII for several reasons. First, section 805(a)(1) of the Act directs the Board to consider relevant international standards in prescribing risk-management standards under Title VIII. As explained in the NPRM, the Core Principles and the CPSS-IOSCO Recommendations were the international standards most relevant to risk management of FMUs.[6] Second, FMUs are familiar with these standards as the long-standing basis for Part I of the Federal Reserve Policy on Payment System Risk ("PSR policy").[7] Third, the Board has significant experience applying these international standards to large-value payment and settlement systems pursuant to its PSR policy.

CPSS and IOSCO recently conducted a comprehensive review of risk-management standards for PCS systems. On April 16, 2012, CPSS and IOSCO issued the final report on the "Principles for Financial Market Infrastructures," which includes an updated, harmonized, and strengthened set of international risk-management standards (the "PFMI").[8] CPSS and IOSCO intend for the PFMI to replace the Core Principles and CPSS-IOSCO Recommendations. As noted in the NPRM, the Board anticipates that it will review the new international standards, consult with other appropriate agencies and the Council, and seek public comment on the adoption of revised standards for designated FMUs based on the new international standards.

Commenters generally appeared to support the Board's approach of using the Core Principles and CPSS-IOSCO Recommendations as a basis for its risk-management standards for designated FMUs under section 805 of the Act. Two commenters explicitly stated their support for the Board's approach. Two other commenters stated that the proposed risk-management standards were largely prudent and sensible.

One commenter was also supportive of the Board's intention to evaluate the new international standards once they are final for the purposes of revising Regulation HH. Two other commenters expressed some general reservations with respect to the new international standards; one of the commenters cautioned the Board against adopting the new international standards "in full," because doing so would include principles that may not directly relate to the risks posed by the designated FMUs and contemplated by Title VIII.

After considering the public comments and for the reasons stated above, the Board continues to believe that the most suitable approach to establishing initial risk-management standards under Title VIII of the Act is to use the Core Principles and CPSS-IOSCO Recommendations as the basis for the standards promulgated by this notice, and to proceed with consideration of the PFMI as the basis for any future revisions. The Board agrees with commenters that international standards that are not, in some way or to some degree, related to existing or potential risks posed to or by a designated FMU should not be adopted for purposes of section 805 of the Act. As noted in the NPRM, the Board acknowledged that the scope of the Core Principles and CPSS-IOSCO Recommendations is broad and proposed to adopt by regulation particular standards, or portions thereof, that relate to the risks presented to or by a designated FMU, rather than those standards, or portions thereof, that apply more generally to financial markets or regulators. Similarly, the Board anticipates evaluating the appropriateness of each of the new PFMI for the purpose of possible revisions to Regulation HH.

2. Applicability of Standards to Retail Payment Systems

Proposed § 234.3 is based on the entire set of the Core Principles. Some commenters questioned whether three standards included in the Core Principles could be applied to retail payment systems, particularly automated clearinghouses ("ACH") and check clearinghouses, should those systems be designated as systemically important by the Council. Specifically, proposed § 234.3(a)(3) would require any FMU that is designated on the basis of its role as operator of a payment system to have clearly defined procedures for the management of credit risks and liquidity risks, which specify the respective responsibilities of the system operator and the participants and which provide appropriate incentives to manage and contain those risks. Proposed § 234.3(a)(4) would require any designated FMU that is designated on the basis of its role as operator of a payment system to provide prompt final settlement on the day of value, preferably during the day and at a minimum at the end of the day. Proposed § 234.3(a)(5) would require any designated FMU that is designated on the basis of its role as operator of a payment system, and in which multilateral netting takes place, to, at a minimum, be capable of ensuring the timely completion of daily settlements in the event of an inability to settle by the participant with the largest single settlement obligation.

The Board received several comments on the applicability of these risk-management standards to retail payment systems, should they be designated by the Council. Several commenters stated their support for an exemption for retail payment systems from designation as systemically important by the Council under the Dodd-Frank Act. The Council, however, determined not to categorically exclude FMUs operating retail payment or other systems in its rule regarding the FMU designation process.[9] As a result, commenters provided feedback on the ability of retail payment systems to meet certain of the Board's proposed risk-management standards in the event the Council decides to designate them.

One commenter specifically referenced proposed § 234.3(a)(3)-(5) as risk-management standards that, while appropriate risk controls for truly systemically important payment systems, were generally inapplicable (or had no relevance) to payments systems such as ACH clearing arrangements that permit the return of transactions within a certain timeframe. One commenter argued that the standard in proposed § 234.3(a)(3) regarding the management of credit and liquidity risk would have no application where a system that did not assume credit and liquidity risks in the first place by committing to pay funds that it had not received and where the payment system participants expect to manage their own credit and liquidity risks. Two commenters also stated that proposed § 234.3(a)(4) on settlement finality contradicts long-standing and established practices of ACH rules that allow for certain transactions to be reversed or returned for any reason until the banking day after the settlement date. One commenter stated that application of proposed § 234.3(a)(5) regarding the ability to complete settlement in the event the single largest participant is unable to settle would require a fundamental change in the nature of ACH debit transactions and the abolishment of the right to return the transaction. In general, these commenters stated that they do not believe that, if designated, retail payment systems would be able to comply with these proposed standards and, accordingly, asked that such systems be exempted from them.

The Board notes that the proposed risk-management standards were designed to apply to large-value payment systems. This approach is consistent with the direction of the Council expressed in its final rule on the FMU designation process. Specifically, the Council stated that, within payment systems, it expects to focus at this time on FMUs that operate large-value systems and not on FMUs that operate low-value systems (such as check and ACH).[10] The Council also decided not to include considerations more narrowly tailored to the characteristics of retail payment systems because the Council did not believe they were necessary or appropriate given the current focus for designations.

Given the Council's focus on large-value systems, the Board does not anticipate that the Council will designate a FMU under Title VIII on the basis of its role as operator of a retail payment system. However, because the authority to designate systemically important FMUs resides with the Council, not the Board, the Board cannot be assured of the type of FMU the Council may designate in the future. In the event that the Council designates an FMU on the basis of its role as operator of a retail payment system, the Board would review, at that time, whether the risk-management standards in § 234.3 were appropriate for that designated FMU, as it would for any type of newly designated FMU.

In order to accommodate this review in the event that an unanticipated type of FMU is designated, and in consideration of the comments, the Board is adopting in the final rule a modification to proposed §§ 234.3(b) and 234.4(b) that clarifies that the application of individual risk-management standards could be waived in a situation where such standards could not appropriately be applied to a particular designated FMU. Both §§ 234.3(b) and 234.4(b) will be amended by inserting text that states "[t]he Board, by order, may waive the application of a standard or standards to a particular designated financial market utility where the risks presented by or the design of that designated financial market utility would make the application of the standard or standards inappropriate." This revision is intended to bridge any gap between Council designation of a new type of designated FMU and the process of promulgating regulations appropriate for the new type of designated FMU, if necessary.

In addition, the Board notes that with respect to a designated FMU that operates more than one payment system (e.g., one large-value and one retail), standards would apply only with respect to the system that provided the basis for the Council's designation of the FMU. The Board is modifying § 234.3(a) and (b) to clarify this point. The Board also is making a parallel modification to § 234.4(a) and (b).[11]

The Board is also modifying §§ 234.3(a) and 234.4(a) to require a designated FMU to "implement rules, procedures, or operations designed to ensure that it meets or exceeds" the risk-management standards set forth in these sections. In addition, the word "should" has been deleted from the individual standards to clarify that these are requirements with which a designated FMU must comply.

3. Scope of Risk-Management Standards

As noted above, the proposed risk-management standards for designated FMUs that operate as payment systems, CCPs, or CSDs are based on the Core Principles and CPSS-IOSCO Recommendations. Each set includes separate standards relating to efficiency, access criteria, and governance. Several commenters suggested that the Board eliminate some or all of these three proposed standards for payment systems, arguing that they address system operating issues that are outside the scope of the systemic risk issues contemplated by Title VIII of the Dodd-Frank Act. Specifically, the commenters questioned whether proposed § 234.3(a)(8), (9), and (10) regarding efficiency, access criteria, and governance, respectively, were relevant to systemic risk.[12] The applicability of the efficiency standard was a common concern of the commenters that raised questions about the scope of the risk-management standards; a subset of these commenters also questioned whether either the access criteria or governance standard was within the scope of risk management. These standards in general were viewed as admirable goals that designated FMUs should aim to achieve, but nevertheless as goals that should be driven by market forces and not by regulatory mandate.

Efficiency. The efficiency standard in proposed § 234.3(a)(8) states that an FMU that is designated on the basis of its role as operator of a payment system should provide a means of making payments that is practical for its users and efficient for the economy. Several commenters argued that the efficiency standard exceeds the Act's objectives because it addresses operating system issues and not risk matters. One commenter argued that whether a form of payment is practical and efficient is largely a matter of judgment that is better left to the market and its participants.

The Board believes the efficiency standard furthers the objectives set out in Title VIII of the Act to reduce systemic risks and support the stability of the broader financial system.

A designated FMU supports the ongoing functioning and stability of the market it serves by providing effective, reliable PCS services to its participants and, in particular, completing timely clearing and settlement of financial transactions. An FMU that is designed or managed inefficiently or impractically may ultimately distort financial activity and market structure, increasing not only the financial and other risks of an FMU's participants, but also the risks of their customers and end users. To avoid such outcomes, a designated FMU should consider the tradeoffs between, and seek a reasonable balance of, safety (i.e., risk management) and efficiency (i.e., direct and indirect costs) when designing and managing the system. For example, overly demanding financial resource requirements may create a liquidity demand so high that it would be impractical for participants to meet. Although liquidity is very important, an FMU that accumulates excessive liquid resources from its participants intraday may increase the participants' opportunity cost of sending each payment. In such cases, participants that become liquidity constrained may be forced to delay submitting certain time- or mission-critical payments.

Additionally, an FMU's design, operating structure, scope of PCS activities, and use of technology can influence its efficiency and can ultimately provide incentives for market participants to use, or not use, the FMU's services. For example, in certain cases, inefficiently designed systems may increase costs to the point where it would be cost-prohibitive for participants to use the FMU, and possibly drive market participants toward less safe alternatives, such as bilateral clearing or settlement on the books of the participants. In such cases, risks to the market participants increase as they seek less safe opportunities to lower direct costs; this behavior may reintroduce risk into the market that the FMU was intended to mitigate.

As these examples suggest, a designated FMU must function efficiently, as well as safely, and provide services that are appropriate to the needs of its users without becoming cost-prohibitive to use. A designated FMU that is inefficient can have a direct, negative impact on financial stability. Accordingly, the Board believes that it is appropriate for a supervisor of a designated FMU to take into account the need for practical and efficient design of the designated FMU as part of the set of risk-management standards set forth in Regulation HH. For these reasons, the Board is adopting the efficiency standards in proposed §§ 234.3(a)(8) and 234.4(a)(6) essentially as set out in the NPRM.

Access criteria. The access criteria standard in proposed § 234.3(a)(9) states that a payment system should have objective and publicly disclosed criteria for participation, which permit fair and open access. Some commenters argued that the access criteria standard did not relate to any of the risks contemplated by Title VIII of the Act. One commenter stated that the actions taken by the payment system, CSD, or CCP, create or mitigate risk, not the rules governing who can participate in them. Another commenter noted that the participation structure for payment systems can vary broadly and, while the participation criteria for these systems could be an issue for competition law, it was difficult to see how the criteria could directly affect the risks that were the focus of Title VIII.

The Board believes that access criteria are important to a designated FMU's risk-management framework and affect the level of risk a designated

FMU presents to the financial system. Access criteria are typically referred to as an FMU's "first line of defense" in ensuring it admits financial institutions that will be able to meet their obligations and not expose the FMU or its other participants to unacceptable risk. Access criteria need to be designed to ensure that participants meet appropriate operational, financial, and legal requirements to allow them to meet their obligations on a timely basis.[13] However, these criteria need to be balanced against the FMU's ability to effectively serve the market it supports, in particular markets that are subject to a statutory requirement for central clearing or settlement through an FMU. Although a designated FMU may use risk-based measures to control access, requirements that are unnecessarily discriminatory or overly restrictive can minimize the FMU's overall effectiveness.

Criteria that allow for fair and open access also may help achieve the Title VIII objectives of reducing systemic risk and supporting the overall stability of the financial system. A fair and open approach to participation criteria may help prevent the concentration of financial activity (and therefore risk) into a few large participants. By encouraging the reduction of risk concentration, the proposed standard helps lower the likelihood that a few financial institutions will be perceived as "too big to fail." Broad participation in a designated FMU can, for example, increase the effectiveness of multilateral netting, facilitate crisis management by applying a consistent set of rules and procedures (e.g., default management, loss mutualization), and improve overall market transparency by increasing the number of transactions processed by the FMU. Accordingly, access criteria that do not permit fair and open access may reduce the overall risk-reduction benefits that a designated FMU can offer.

For these reasons, the Board is adopting the access criteria standards in proposed §§ 234.3(a)(9) and 234.4(a)(2) essentially as set out in the NPRM.

Governance. The governance standard in proposed § 234.3(a)(10) states that a payment system's governance arrangements should be effective, accountable, and transparent. Some commenters claimed that although the decisions made by a designated FMU's governing body can affect the risks it presents, the particular governance structure itself presents no such risks. Conversely, one commenter supported inclusion of the governance standard, stating that weak governance practices and poor risk-management procedures at designated FMUs could pose hazards both to participating financial institutions and to the market as a whole. Another commenter stated that risk management effectively encompasses governance, among other areas.

The Board believes that effective, accountable, and transparent governance arrangements are critical to the effective risk management of a designated FMU. A strong governance arrangement provides a sound basis for compliance with the other risk-management standards in Regulation HH. A number of tools or techniques discussed in the Core Principles with respect to the governance standard have proved to be effective in ensuring effective governance, such as written strategic objectives and plans for achieving them and separation of risk management and audit functions from day-to-day operations. The Board expects supervisors to review a designated FMU's governance arrangements against the background of these and other relevant techniques in order to promote robust risk management. In addition, given the role of the FMU's board of directors in setting the overall risk-management framework of the designated FMU, the Board believes that a weak or ineffective governance structure could have systemic implications for the participants of the service, other FMUs, and other markets. Accordingly, the Board believes that a supervisor should consider a designated FMU's governance arrangements when performing its systemic risk review. For these reasons, the Board is adopting the governance standard in proposed §§ 234.3(a)(10) and 234.4(a)(8) essentially as set out in the NPRM.

4. Independent Model Validation

Proposed § 234.4(a)(17) requires a designated FMU that operates as a CCP to use margin requirements to limit its credit exposures to participants in normal market conditions and use risk-based models and parameters that are reviewed regularly. In addition, proposed § 234.4(a)(17)(i) would require a CCP to provide for annual model validation consisting of evaluating the performance of the CCP's margin models and the related parameters and assumptions associated with such models by a qualified person who does not perform functions associated with the CCP's margin models (except as part of the annual model validation) and also does not report to such a person.[14] Two commenters noted that proposed § 234.4(a)(17)(i), although on the right track, should stress explicitly the complete independence of the organization conducting the validation. One of the commenters believed models must be validated annually by a qualified and independent organization with no financial stake in the outcome because no employee of a systemically important CCP should be expected to resist the inevitable direct and indirect pressures of management who may have incentives to achieve a less-appropriate and less-independent outcome. The other commenter also stated that model validation must be performed by a truly independent party with no financial stake in the outcome of the validation and expressed concern that a validator that is not sufficiently independent would face the conflict of interest that would lead designated FMUs to lower their margins in order to attract business and increase profits.

The Board believes that a validator must be able to offer independent, unbiased conclusions and recommendations as part of the margin model validation process. It is unlikely that the person who was responsible for initially developing the margin model would be able to provide an independent, unbiased assessment of the product. Similarly, it appears unlikely that a person under the functional control of the developer would be able to provide independent, unbiased validation of the model without the influence of the developer and concern for employment security. Accordingly, proposed § 234.4(a)(17)(i) would require that the model validation be conducted by a qualified person who does not perform functions associated with the CCP's margin model, such as development and implementation, and does not report to such a person.[15]

The Board recognizes the concern expressed in the comments that there may be financial considerations beyond the validator's immediate employment security, and that there may be situations where a validator from outside the CCP may be needed to provide an appropriately independent validation. In such cases, the Board may hold a particular designated FMU to a stricter definition of independent validation that is appropriate for the level of risk presented by the designated FMU. Proposed § 234.4(b) allows for the Board, by order, to apply heightened risk-management standards to a particular designated FMU in response to the risks presented by that designated FMU. As a generally applicable standard, however, the Board believes it is appropriate to recognize basic requirements for an independent validation. For these reasons, the Board is adopting proposed § 234.4(a)(17)(i) essentially as set out in the NPRM.

5. Financial Resource Coverage

Proposed § 234.4(a)(15) would require a designated FMU that is acting as a CSD to institute risk controls that include collateral requirements and limits, and ensure timely settlement in the event that the participant with the largest payment obligation is unable to settle when the CSD extends intraday credit. Proposed § 234.4(a)(18) would require a designated FMU that is acting as a CCP to maintain sufficient financial resources to withstand, at a minimum, a default by the participant to which it has the largest exposure in extreme but plausible market conditions. The Board specifically requested comment on whether such designated FMUs should be required to maintain sufficient financial resources to withstand the default by the participant with the largest exposure or obligation in extreme but plausible market conditions, where the "participant" means the family of affiliated participants when there is more than one affiliated participant ("cover one"), or whether such designated FMUs should be required to maintain sufficient financial resources to withstand the defaults by the two participants, plus any affiliated participants, with the largest exposures or obligations in extreme but plausible market conditions ("cover two").

Two commenters stated that, if the Board continued to base its financial resources standard on the number of participants that pose large risk exposures to a CCP, they supported the higher cover two requirement. One commenter cited the "interconnectedness of financial institutions" as one of the central dangers, which must be addressed by financial reforms and a reason for adopting a cover two standard. This commenter also suggested that the Board's rule should conform to a similar standard proposed by the CFTC for systemically important DCOs, which included a cover two requirement.[16] The other commenter supported a cover two standard because, during a period of extreme market stress, it cannot be guaranteed that there will be only a single default. Neither commenter, however, provided any analysis to support its contention that a cover two standard would be more appropriate as a generally applicable standard.

Both commenters, however, expressed a preference for a financial resource coverage requirement based on an additional measurement as determined by a percentage of aggregate exposure, and suggested that the default rate used in stress tests be based on the larger of (a) the two members representing the largest exposure to the CCP and (b) the members constituting at least 33 percent of the exposures in aggregate to the CCP. The two commenters believed that the additional measurement captures the risk of a diverse, but interconnected, membership.

As noted in the NPRM, the Board's proposed financial resources standards would apply a heightened cover one requirement because the term "participant" would be interpreted as the largest family of affiliated participants if there was more than one affiliated participant. The Board believes that this interpretation will address the interconnectedness of participants through corporate ownership structures. With respect to risks presented by other types of interconnectedness (i.e., through common participation across markets or FMUs), the standards for a designated FMU's financial resource coverage, as with all other standards set out in the regulation, are generally applicable standards. The Board expects that a designated FMU would employ a risk-management framework that is appropriate for the risks faced by the FMU and the FMU may, at its own initiative, institute a cover two financial resource coverage requirement. In addition, the Board may require, by order, a particular designated FMU to exceed the generally applicable standards set out in the regulation to address the risks presented by, including those borne by, the FMU.[17] Although the existing cover one standard was adopted by the Board in its PSR policy and applied in its supervision of payment and settlement systems since 1994, the Board has applied heightened financial resource coverage requirements when the appropriate situation arose. Therefore, although the Board agrees with the commenters that, in some cases, a higher requirement would be more appropriate to the level of risk presented by a particular designated FMU, the Board believes, at this time, that the most appropriate course is to adopt the cover one standard as generally applicable and impose a higher standard, including possibly a cover two standard, on a case-by-case basis when appropriate. The Board will consider the appropriateness of adopting a cover two standard in the context of possible revisions to Regulation HH in light of the PFMI. Accordingly, the Board is adopting the cover one standard in § 234.4(a)(15) and (18) essentially as set out in the NPRM.

The Board believes the commenters' concern regarding appropriately addressing the interconnectedness of a designated FMU's participants and the suggestion of applying the additional measurement using a percentage of aggregate exposure are important to consider. Before determining the viability of this approach, however, the Board believes further analysis is needed regarding how the suggested additional measure would be applied, and such analysis could include identifying situations in which the additional aggregate exposure measure would capture risk that is not addressed by either a cover one or cover two standard, an explanation of how the additional measure would be calculated (including the appropriate time horizon to use), and an explanation of why a 33 percent aggregate exposure standard would be most appropriate for this approach. The Board will consider this approach further in the context of revisions to Regulation HH in light of the PFMI. The Board welcomes and will review any supporting research on this issue that is submitted.

6. Legal Certainty of Netting Arrangements

One commenter raised an issue regarding designated FMUs that allow netting of payments to and from individual participants. The commenter stated that, to ensure that the netting will be honored in a bankruptcy or other insolvency proceeding, Regulation HH must require that the designated FMU demonstrate that, under the policies, procedures, and documentation of the designated FMU, the netting permitted by the designated FMU will be given legal effect in default and insolvency situations through an analysis provided by outside legal counsel that is a nationally recognized expert in matters of corporate insolvency.

The Board recognizes the importance of legal certainty of a designated FMU's transactions, not only during default and insolvency situations, but also at all other times. To address these concerns, the Board proposed standards regarding a designated FMU's legal framework for payment systems, as well as CSDs and CCPs. For example, proposed § 234.4(a)(1) states that the CSD or CCP should have a well-founded, transparent, and enforceable legal framework for each aspect of its activities in all relevant jurisdictions. As explained in the NPRM, the Board expects that a designated FMU will manage its legal risks within the context of currently applicable statutes and regulations, so it can ensure that its rules, procedures, and contractual provisions will be enforceable with a high degree of certainty.[18]

Legal certainty of each aspect of a designated FMU's activities (including its netting function) is expected to be supported by existing law in all relevant jurisdictions. Obtaining an opinion of outside counsel is one method for a designated FMU to judge legal certainty of its rules and procedures, but it is not the only method. In many cases, the designated FMU's in-house counsel may be better positioned to evaluate the intricacies of the designated FMU's netting arrangements and the law of the jurisdictions that are relevant to the designated FMU's operations. In addition, obtaining an opinion of outside counsel could involve significant expense for the designated FMU, depending on the complexity and number of relevant jurisdictions. The Board does not believe it is appropriate to impose such costs as a general expectation when they may not be necessary in all cases. Whether legal certainty must be supported by an opinion of outside counsel or may be verified by in-house counsel is a decision that may be made initially by management of the designated FMU. In the event the Board determines in a particular situation that an opinion by outside counsel is warranted, it could require such an opinion in that case. For these reasons, the Board believes that the legal framework standard as proposed is sufficient to address the concerns raised by the commenter.

7. Costs of Risk-Management Standards to Participants

One commenter urged the Board to ensure that the benefits of enhanced risk-management standards exceed the costs of implementing the standards on banks and their customers. The commenter stated that banks will feel the effects of the risk-management standards because any designated FMUs with whom the banks transact business will likely pass on the costs and constraints of enhanced supervisory oversight to their participants.

The Board is keenly aware of the need to weigh the costs and benefits of particular rulemakings. Section 805(a) of the Act requires the Board to prescribe risk-management standards governing the operations related to the PCS activities of designated FMUs. The Board's discretion lies not in whether risk-management standards must be promulgated, but rather in how the Board can best avoid unnecessary burden associated with the standards.

With respect to the benefits of the risk-management standards, section 805(b) states that the objectives and principles for the standards are to (1) Promote robust risk management; (2) promote safety and soundness; (3) reduce systemic risks; and (4) support the stability of the broader financial system. The benefit of reducing systemic risk is, of course, difficult to quantify. Generally speaking, however, an FMU that is better positioned to withstand disruptive systemic events would result in much smaller costs being borne by the FMU, and its participants, and, more generally, the financial system and taxpayers.

The costs of the risk-management standards can be viewed as a designated FMU's incremental expenses in establishing and maintaining the systems and procedures necessary to meet the standards, and other Regulation HH requirements, over and above the risk-management measures the FMU would have otherwise adopted for business reasons. As the commenter noted, such costs are generally passed on to a designated FMU's participants. These costs could take the form of higher transaction costs, margin or collateral costs, and capital requirements. These costs should be weighed against the societal benefit of stability in the financial system and the economy more broadly.

As explained in the NPRM, the Board proposed to adopt the Core Principles and CPSS-IOSCO Recommendations as the basis for the risk-management standards required by the Act, in part because that approach strikes a reasonable balance between furthering the Act's goals of enhanced risk management and financial stability and controlling the costs imposed on the FMUs. As explained in the NPRM, the Core Principles and CPSS-IOSCO Recommendations were formulated by central banks and securities regulators over several years and with considerable discussion and input from the financial services industry. The Federal Reserve collaborated with participating financial system authorities in developing the three sets of standards. In addition, the SEC and CFTC participated in the development of the CPSS-IOSCO Recommendations. The three sets of standards, particularly those relevant to payment systems, have been incorporated into the Board's PSR policy for many years. Further, the Board has used these standards, in conjunction with relevant laws and other Federal Reserve policies, when exercising its authority with respect to supervising payment and securities settlement systems.[19] FMUs that are likely to be designated by the Council, as well as their participants, are well-acquainted with these standards and, in many cases, such FMUs have already incorporated these standards into their governance, risk-management, and operating frameworks. The Board, therefore, does not anticipate material additional costs associated with adopting the Core Principles and CPSS-IOSCO Recommendations into its regulation for participants in payment systems already managing towards these standards.

Although these standards would be generally applicable, the Board is retaining the authority to impose a more stringent standard or waive a standard on a case-by-case basis in situations where it is warranted.[20] The Board believes this is a more cost-effective approach to achieving the risk management objectives of Title VIII of the Act. For example, when a situation that warrants a higher standard is discovered, the Board will exercise its authority to tailor a higher standard for the risks presented. In addition, alternatively, if review of the PFMI demonstrates that a higher standard is more appropriate for general application, the Board will consider a revision to the regulation.

B. Advance Notice of Material Changes

1. Materiality Threshold

Section 806(e) of the Act requires a designated FMU to provide 60 days' advance notice to its Supervisory Agency of any proposed change to its rules, procedures, or operations "that could, as defined in rules of each Supervisory Agency, materially affect the nature or level of risks presented" by the designated FMU. Proposed § 234.5(c)(1) states that the term "materially affect the nature or level of risks presented" means matters as to which there is a "reasonable possibility that the change could materially affect the performance of clearing, settlement, or payment functions or the overall nature or level of risk presented by the designated financial market utility." Proposed § 234.5(c)(2) provides a non-exclusive list of changes that would materially affect the nature or level of risks presented, including changes that affect participant eligibility or access criteria; product eligibility; risk management; settlement failure or default procedures; financial resources; business continuity and disaster recovery plans; daily or intraday settlement procedures; scope of services; non-routine changes to the underlying technological framework for PCS functions; or governance. Proposed § 234.5(c)(3) provides a non-exclusive list of changes that would not materially affect the nature or level of risks presented, including a change that does not modify the contractual rights or obligations of the designated FMU or its participants; a change that does not adversely affect the safeguarding of securities, collateral, or funds for which the designated FMU is responsible; a routine technology upgrade; a routine administrative change; or a non-substantive change to rules, procedures, or other documentation.

The Board requested comments on all aspects of its proposed materiality rule, particularly on the appropriateness of the definition of "materially affect the nature or level of risks presented" and the utility of the non-exclusive lists for material and non-material changes. Commenters generally stated that the materiality standard would benefit from one or more of the following three adjustments: (1) A narrower scope of the definition itself, (2) a shorter list of inclusions, or (3) a more expansive list of exclusions.

"Reasonable possibility." Several commenters stated that the definition of "materially affect the nature or level of risks presented" is overly vague and were concerned that the Board would be flooded with advance notices of non-material changes as a result. Three commenters generally stated that the definition of materiality is too vague and suggest a more narrowly drawn definition to provide for expeditious review. One commenter suggested revising the proposed materiality standard, which requires notice of proposed changes that have "a reasonable possibility" of material effect, to require notice only for those changes that are "reasonably likely" to have a material effect. The commenter stated that, with the proposed definition, designated FMUs were highly likely to err in favor of significantly "over-disclosing" changes to their rules, procedures, and operations, which would be overly burdensome to both the Board and the industry.

The Board believes the proposed definition sets an appropriate minimum threshold for advance notices at this time. Proposed § 234.5(c) asks the designated FMU to consider whether it is reasonably possible that a change could have a material effect on the performance of its PCS functions or its overall risk profile. The Board recognizes that "possible" is a lower threshold than "likely." Section 806(e)(1) of the Act uses the phrase "could *** materially affect" the PCS functions or its overall risk profile of the designated

FMU. This word choice indicates possibility, rather than likelihood.[21] If Congress had intended that advance notices be submitted only for changes that were likely to have a material effect, it could easily have framed it in that way. In addition, when the Board seeks to fulfill its statutory responsibility, the lower threshold is appropriate to ensure that it is able to review a broad sampling of the types of material changes that the designated FMU normally makes in its operations. As the designated FMU submits advance notices, the Board will be able to provide feedback and filter out the specific types of rule changes normally considered by that particular designated FMU that do not warrant advance notices. Within this framework, the Board anticipates that it will be able to more precisely balance the regulatory burden of the advance notice requirement with its need to receive advance notice of material changes for the supervision of a particular designated FMU contemplated by Title VIII of the Act.

Further, the suggested revision would require the designated FMU to determine which changes were likely to materially affect the performance of its PCS functions or its overall risk profile. Making this judgment without any input from the Board would increase the risk that the designated FMU would not submit an advance notice to the Board that the Board would determine could have a material effect. This not only could subject the designated FMU to supervisory criticism and possible modification or rescission of the change, but also could prevent the Board from obtaining valuable insight into the operations of the designated FMU as contemplated by the statute.

Although a lower materiality threshold initially may result in a higher number of advance notice filings, the Board does not believe that this is a reason to change the definition. The Board will provide guidance, through ongoing dialogue during the supervisory process, to assist a designated FMU in determining whether a proposed change requires advanced notice. For the reasons set out above, the Board is retaining the "reasonable possibility" language in the definition of "materially affect the nature or level of risks presented" in § 234.5(c)(1) of the final rule.

"Performance of clearing, settlement, or payment functions." One commenter suggested deleting from the materiality definition the phrase "performance of clearing, settlement, or payment functions." The commenter stated that the proposed definition of materiality overreaches the statutory purpose of ensuring sound risk management by requiring advance notice of changes that affect the performance of PCS functions in addition to the overall nature or level or risks presented. The commenter stated that changes implemented by the designated FMU that relate to the broad category of

"performance," as opposed to risk, are more appropriately vetted in the competitive marketplace.

In referring to the performance of PCS functions, the Board intended to provide additional guidance to the scope of the advance notice requirement by including an express focus on the PCS functions of a designated FMU. The Board believes that the language in proposed § 234.5(c)(1) appropriately implements the statutory authority provided by the Act. To address the commenters' concerns and provide clarity regarding the scope of the advance notice requirement in § 234.5(c)(1), the Board is adopting a revision to the proposed regulatory text to state that the term "materially affect the nature or level of risks presented" means matters as to which there is a reasonable possibility that the change could "materially affect the overall nature or level of risk presented by the designated financial market utility, including risk arising in the performance of payment, clearing, or settlement functions." [22] This revision ensures that the definition follows the statutory authority, while also providing an indication that the Board expects designated FMUs to pay particular attention to providing advance notice of proposed changes to its rules, procedures, or operations regarding the performance of its PCS functions that could materially affect the nature or level of risks presented by the designated FMU. The additional guidance, however, does not limit the scope of "materially affect the nature or level of risks presented" to only those risks arising in the performance of PCS functions. A proposed change to any of the designated FMU's rules, procedures, or operations that could materially affect the nature or level of risks presented by the designated FMU should be the subject of an advance notice, regardless of whether it is regarding the performance of PCS functions.

Non-exclusive lists. Four commenters stated that the non-exclusive list of material changes in proposed § 234.5(c)(2) was too broad or the non-exclusive list of non-material changes in proposed § 234.5(c)(3) was too narrow. The commenters acknowledged the value of providing guidance regarding changes that were material or not material, but generally stated that the proposed lists did not appropriately draw this dividing line.

One commenter stated that most items included on the material list in proposed § 234.5(c)(2) are described in a manner that would require a designated FMU to provide the Board notice of changes that would not necessarily affect the nature or level of risk in any manner. In particular, the commenter noted that "financial resources" is included in the list in proposed § 234.5(c)(2)(v), but is not modified by any quantitative or qualitative measure, so a designated FMU would be required to submit advance notice of any change in its financial resources, even changes that are not material, such as any changes that in any way affect capital, access to credit, or liquidity. Two commenters cited the "scope of services" item in proposed § 234.5(c)(2)(viii) as another example of an overly broad requirement that is unrelated to risk. For similar reasons, two commenters suggested deleting the "governance" item in proposed § 234.5(c)(2)(x). One commenter also suggested deleting the "participant eligibility or access" item in proposed § 234.5(c)(2)(i).

The Board believes that material changes in the areas listed in proposed § 234.5(c)(2) could affect a designated FMU's core functions and, as a result, might affect its ability to manage its risks appropriately and to continue to conduct systemically important PCS services. This may, in turn, affect the designated FMU's ability to comply with the risk-management standards set out in §§ 234.3 and 234.4 to which they will be held. The list of material changes provided in proposed § 234.5(c)(2) was intended to track those risk-management standards, and the reasons for including these items in the list of material changes requiring an advance notice are similar in most cases. For example, the importance of understanding material changes in the financial resources of a designated FMU acting as a payment system would be critical to assessing the ability of the designated FMU to continue to provide systemically important PCS services in the event of a default, as well as its compliance with several of the proposed risk-management standards, such as the capability to ensure timely completion of daily settlements as set out in proposed § 234.3(a)(5).

To address the commenters' concerns that de minimis changes to the areas listed in § 234.5(c)(2) would require an advance notice, the Board is adopting revised language in the final rule to clarify that the changes that "materially affect" the areas listed would be considered changes that materially affect the nature or level of risks presented by the designated FMU.

Also, as explained above regarding the risk-management standard for governance in proposed § 234.3(a)(10), the Board believes that effective, accountable, and transparent governance arrangements are critical to effective risk management of a designated FMU. As a result, changes that materially affect a designated FMU's governance arrangements should be submitted pursuant to the advance notice process.

Similarly, the Board believes that access criteria can help ensure that a designated FMU admits financial institutions that will be able to meet their obligations and not expose the FMU or its other participants to risk, including through risk measures such as capital ratios, risk ratings, or other indicators. For this reason, the Board will have an interest in receiving advance notice of any material changes to a designated FMU's participant eligibility or access criteria. Finally, understanding the scope of services offered by an FMU that is designated on the basis of its role as operator of a payment system is fundamental to being able to have a clear understanding of the payment system's risk profile. A designated FMU's services could affect the financial risks participants face through their participation in the system, as well as the level of risk that the designated FMU is incurring by providing the services.

Commenters also suggested revising the list of non-material changes in proposed § 234.5(c)(3).[23] One commenter stated that certain examples on the non-material list are so narrowly drawn as to be unhelpful in marking a reasonable line between circumstances that may compel advance notice and those that may not. As an example, the commenter cited the example of "a change that does not modify the contractual rights or obligations of the designated financial market utility or persons using its payment, clearing, or settlement services" set out in proposed § 234.5(c)(3)(i) and noted these types of changes, in essence, would be the types of clerical, non-substantive changes separately identified in proposed § 234.5(c)(3)(v). Another commenter supported a broad application of the example set forth in § 234.5(c)(3)(ii) ("a change to an existing procedure, control, or service that does not adversely affect the safeguarding of securities, collateral, or funds in the custody or control of the designated financial market utility or for which it is responsible").

After taking into consideration the comments noted above and reexamining the list of non-material changes, the Board is eliminating the examples in proposed §§ 234.5(c)(3)(i) and (ii). With respect to proposed § 234.5(c)(3)(i), the Board recognizes the commenter's concern; however, the Board believes it is more prudent to capture a wider range of proposed changes at this time and therefore is reluctant to expand the example's breadth. In addition, the Board is concerned that a broad application of the non-material change set forth in proposed § 234.5(c)(3)(ii) might inadvertently create an overlap with the advance notice requirement for material change set forth in § 234.5(c)(2)(iii) because both changes fall broadly within the area of risk management. In order to avoid this overlap, and any resulting confusion, the Board is removing the example in proposed § 234.5(c)(3)(ii).

The list provided by the Board in § 234.5(c)(3) is not meant to be exhaustive. The Board believes that it is difficult to draw a bright line that could be uniformly applicable to all designated FMUs between changes that would require advance notice and those that would not because of the range of different designs and functions. The Board believes, at this time, that routine changes like those listed in the remaining examples of § 234.5(c)(3) would be considered clearly non-material for the purposes of triggering the 60-day advance notice requirement. In addition, the Board believes that changes to fees, prices, or other charges for services provided by the designated FMU constitute business decisions that would not require advance notice. To that end, the Board is adopting an explicit exclusion for fees, prices, or other charges in § 234.5(c)(3)(ii). As mentioned above, as the supervisory process develops with a particular designated FMU, the Board anticipates that it will reach an understanding with the FMU about what constitutes a non-material rule change for that FMU that would not require advance notice.

2. Expedited Review

Proposed § 234.5(a) includes procedural requirements regarding advance notices of material changes, such as the required content of the notices and the procedures and timing for the methods for approving such changes. These provisions essentially reiterate similar provisions in section 806(e) of the Dodd-Frank Act. Some commenters were concerned that the open-ended time frame for the Board to request additional information on a material change would unnecessarily delay action on certain changes to rules, procedures, or operations that are time sensitive, but do not materially affect the level of risks posed by the designated FMU. As a means of expediting the processing of advance notice submissions, commenters made several suggestions to limit the time of the Board's review, such as (a) establishing a 10-day preliminary determination window in which the Board determines whether a proposed change requires advance notice or a full 60-day review and (b) limiting the Board's authority to request additional information to assess the effects of the proposed change to within the first 30 days of the review period. The commenters were generally concerned that the Board would engage in an indefinite and extended review of advance notices that would hinder a designated FMU's ability to manage its business.

As a general matter, the Board recognizes the importance of reducing regulatory burden and being diligent in reviewing proposed material changes in a timely manner. Section 806(e)(1)(I) of the Act permits a designated FMU to implement a change in less than 60 days from the filing of the advance notice if its Supervisory Agency notifies the designated FMU that it does not object to the proposed change and authorizes the designated FMU to implement the change at an earlier date. The Board incorporated this statutory provision in proposed § 234.5(a)(8) and is retaining this provision in the final rule. This provision provides a mechanism for the Board to complete its review and inform the designated FMU that it may proceed before the expiration of the 60-day advance notice period. The Board expects to use this procedure as appropriate. The Board, however, recognizes that it must balance the need for expediency with the need to conduct a thorough review of any necessary supporting documentation or information related to a proposed change, in order to make an informed decision consistent with its statutory responsibilities. Therefore, the timeliness of the Board's review may depend, in part, on the completeness of the information provided by and level of engagement with the designated FMU prior to and following the submission of the advance notice.

3. Advance Notice by Rule-Setting Bodies

Two commenters responsible for developing and setting rules for retail payment systems suggested that the Board's advance notice procedure permit the submission of a proposed rule change by the rule-writing body and that such submission satisfy the advance notice requirement for any designated payment system operating subject to the rules. As an initial matter, the Board will be mindful of the need for efficiency and minimizing regulatory burden, while also ensuring that the Board receives the necessary information on a timely basis in order to fulfill its responsibilities under the Act. The Board notes, however, that although such rule-writing arrangements exist for several retail payment networks, as noted above, such systems are not expected to be designated by the Council as systemically important at this time. If the Council designates any payment systems subject to such rule-writing arrangements and the Board is the Supervisory Agency for that system, the Board would review, at that time, the appropriate means for such systems to submit advance notices.

4. Emergency Changes

One commenter requested that the Board take care in allowing designated FMUs to make immediate emergency changes to their governing rules under proposed § 234.5(b), particularly with respect to customer collateral and margin requirements. The commenter stated that situations that justify alteration of loss mutualization standards from international standards are rare and should be carefully scrutinized. The commenter also requested that the Board incorporate CPSS-IOSCO principles with regard to customer collateral and margin requirements so as to ensure that designated FMUs will apply loss mutualization standards that comport with international standards.

Section 806(e)(2) of the Act contemplates the possibility that designated FMUs may need to implement material changes to their rules, procedures, or operations in emergency situations and includes a mechanism allowing for the ex-post notification of the Supervisory Agency regarding such emergency material changes. This mechanism was incorporated into proposed § 234.5(b). In order to take advantage of the emergency change process, a designated FMU is required to explain to the Board within 24 hours of the implementation of the change, among other things, the nature of the emergency and the reason the changes was necessary for the designated FMU to continue to provide its services in a safe and sound manner. Pursuant to Title VIII and the proposed rule, the Board may require modification or rescission of the change if it finds that the change is not consistent with the purposes of the Act or rules or standards prescribed thereunder. The Board expects that emergency changes, including any changes to customer collateral and margin requirements, will occur rarely and will be carefully scrutinized.

5. Advance Notice and Competitive Issues

Two commenters raised concerns regarding the advance notice procedure for designated FMUs that offer services that compete with services offered by the Federal Reserve Banks ("Reserve Banks"). One commenter involved in check imaging stated that if Reserve Banks engaged in check image services were not subject to the advance notice procedure under proposed § 234.5(a) and private-sector check-image-exchange rules were subject to the advance notice procedure, the Reserve Banks would enjoy a significant competitive advantage over the private-sector competitors. This commenter believed that the Reserve Banks would be able to change their check-image rules without being subject to the same delay and uncertainty as the competing designated FMU under the advance notice procedure. The commenter suggested that the Board include within the final rule provisions that seek to mitigate the potential for a negative impact on competition that may arise from the advance notice procedure for designated FMUs. Another commenter stated that it was beyond the scope of systemic risk regulation for the Board to "force a delay in implementing business-related changes; particularly in a competitive market in which the Reserve Banks offer the competing alternative."

The Board is cognizant of the competition between the Reserve Banks and private-sector service providers in certain financial services, including check and funds transfer services, and has long-standing policies to address such competitive issues. Under the Federal Reserve Act, the Board has general supervisory authority over the Reserve Banks, including the Reserve Banks' provision of payment and settlement services ("Reserve Bank financial services"), that is much more extensive in scope than the authority provided under Title VIII over designated FMUs.[24] In practice, Board oversight of the Reserve Banks in many ways goes beyond the typical supervisory framework for private-sector entities, including the framework provided by Title VIII. For example, the Board applies robust risk-management standards to the relevant Reserve Bank financial services; conducts regular examinations; and reviews key strategic initiatives, prices and service terms, proposed material changes, and ongoing operations.

The Board conducts regular examinations of the Reserve Bank financial services covering, among other things, operational safety and soundness and management effectiveness. It also regularly monitors the services' operations and initiatives through reports, discussions with Reserve Bank management, and its oversight liaison roles on various Reserve Bank management groups. The Board is also involved in reviewing or approving proposed changes to the Reserve Banks' rules, procedures, and operations, including those involving Reserve Bank financial services, from their inception. The Board's oversight of these proposed changes is significantly broader and more detailed than the Title VIII advance notice procedures. For example, the Board reviews all changes to the Reserve Banks' operating circulars, approves the Reserve Banks' budgets, including budgets related to the Reserve Bank financial services, and approves major strategic initiatives, and the associated expenditures.

Moreover, the Board recognizes the critical role Reserve Bank financial services, particularly the Fedwire Funds and Fedwire Securities services, play in the financial system and is committed to strong and effective supervision of these services that is comparable to, or exceeds, the requirements placed on similar private-sector entities. For example, the Board expects the Fedwire services to meet or exceed the Board's PSR policy standards, which are consistent with the Regulation HH standards applied to designated FMUs. In addition, the Board will hold the Reserve Banks to advance notice requirements with respect to proposed material changes to Fedwire rules, procedures, and operations that are the same as, or higher than, the requirements for designated FMUs that are supervised by the Board.[25] Moreover, if the Council designates an FMU on the basis of its role as operator of a payment system that competes with another Reserve Bank service, the Board will ensure that the competing Reserve Bank service is held to the same or higher requirements as those set forth in Regulation HH.

In addition, in order to address any competitive inequalities between Reserve Bank priced services and similar services provided by private sector entities, the Monetary Control Act of 1980 (the "MCA") requires Reserve

Bank priced services to be priced explicitly and that fees be established on basis of all direct and indirect costs actually incurred, including taxes that would have been paid and a return on capital that would have been provided had the services been furnished by a private business firm.[26] As required by the MCA, the Board also has established a set of pricing principles that governs the schedule of fees for the Reserve Bank priced services, which must give due regard to competitive factors.[27] Board policy also requires that Federal Reserve actions are implemented in a manner that ensures fairness to other providers of payment services.[28] In light of these policies, the Board believes that changes to Reserve Bank priced services rules or operating circulars are subject to no less scrutiny, and in many cases more scrutiny, than the review contemplated by Title VIII's advance notice procedure.

III. Administrative Law Matters

A. Regulatory Flexibility Act Analysis

The Regulatory Flexibility Act (5 U.S.C. 601 *et seq.*) ("RFA") generally requires an agency to perform an initial and a final regulatory flexibility analysis on the impact a rule is expected to have on small entities. However, under section 605(b) of the RFA, the regulatory flexibility analysis otherwise required under section 604 of the RFA is not required if an agency certifies, along with a statement providing the factual basis for such certification, that the rule will not have a significant economic impact on a substantial number of small entities. Based on current information, the Board believes that the payment systems that would likely be designated by the Council would not be "small entities" for purposes of the RFA, and so, the final rule likely would not have a significant economic impact on a substantial number of small entities. The authority to designate FMUs, however, resides with the Council, rather than the Board, and the Board therefore cannot be assured of the identity of the FMUs that the Council may designate in the future. Accordingly, the Board has prepared the following final regulatory flexibility analysis pursuant to section 604 of the RFA.

1. *Statement of the need for, and objectives of, the final rule.* In accordance with Sections 805(a) and 806(e) of the Dodd-Frank Act, the Board is adopting the final rule as Regulation HH, new Part 234 of Title 12 of the Code of Federal Regulations. The final rule establishes risk-management standards for systemically important FMUs and standards for determining

when advance notice is required to be provided by a designated FMU that proposes to change to its rules, procedures, or operations that could materially affect the nature or level of risks presented by the designated financial market utility. The reasons and justification for the final rule are described above in the Supplementary Information.

2. *Summary of the significant issues raised by public comment on Board's initial analysis, the Board's assessment of such issues, and a statement of any changes made as a result of such comments.* The Board did not receive any public comments regarding its initial regulatory flexibility analysis.

3. *Small entities affected by the final rule.* The final rule would affect FMUs that the Council designates as systemically important to the U.S. financial system for which the Board is the Supervisory Agency. The Board estimates that fewer than five large-value payment systems would meet these conditions and be affected by this rule. Pursuant to regulations issued by the Small Business Administration (the "SBA") (13 CFR 121.201), a "small entity" includes an establishment engaged in providing financial transaction processing, reserve and liquidity services, or clearinghouse services with an average revenue of $7 million or less (NAICS code 522320). As noted in the NPRM, the Board does not currently believe that any of the payment systems that would likely be designated by the Council would be "small entities" pursuant to the SBA regulation. In addition, the Board does not believe at this time that, pursuant to section 803(8) of the Dodd-Frank Act, it would be the Supervisory Agency for any FMU that operates as a central securities depository or central counterparty and that would likely be designated by the Council.

4. *Recordkeeping, reporting, and compliance requirements.* The final rule imposes certain reporting and recordkeeping requirements for a designated FMU. (See, for example, § 234.3(a)(3) (requiring clearly defined procedures for the management of credit risks and liquidity risks); § 234.5(a)(1) and (2) (requiring advance notice of changes that could materially affect the nature or level of risks presented by the designated FMU), and § 234.5(b)(2) and (3) (requiring notice of an emergency change implemented by a designated FMU).) The final rule also contains a number of compliance requirements, including the standards that the designated FMU must meet, such as having a well-founded legal basis under all relevant jurisdictions and having rules and procedures that enable participants to understand clearly the FMU's impact on each of the financial risks they incur by participation in it. Payment systems under the Board's jurisdiction (including certain payment systems the Board believes could be designated as systemically important) are generally already

expected to meet these standards, or are at least familiar with these standards, so the rule would not likely impose material additional costs on those payment systems.

5. *Significant alternatives to the revisions.* Section 805(a) of the Act requires the Board to prescribe risk-management standards governing the operations related to PCS activities of designated FMUs, so other administrative methods for accomplishing the goals of the Act were not considered. One alternative to adopting risk-management standards based on the relevant international standards was to develop a different set of risk-management standards specifically for purposes of section 805(a) of the Act. As explained in the NPRM and above, the Board proposed to adopt the Core Principles and CPSS-IOSCO Recommendations as the basis for establishing initial risk-management standards required by section 805(a) of the Act, in part, because this approach presented advantageous cost efficiencies for the regulators and the FMUs. Furthermore, the new standards set forth in the PFMI were still under development at the time of the NPRM and not available for consideration as an alternative. As explained above, the Core Principles and CPSS-IOSCO Recommendations were formulated by central banks and securities regulators with considerable discussion and industry consultation. In particular, the Federal Reserve collaborated with participating financial system authorities and consulted with FMUs and their participants in developing the standards. In addition, the SEC and CFTC participated in the development of the CPSS-IOSCO Recommendations. The Board incorporated these standards in its PSR policy in 2004 and 2007 and has been guided by the policy, in conjunction with relevant laws and other Federal Reserve policies, when exercising its authority with respect to supervising large-value payment and securities settlement systems.[29] Payment systems that would likely be designated by the Council, therefore, would likely be familiar with the Core Principles and could implement them promptly with relatively less burden than if the Board developed a different set of standards to implement section 805(a) of the Act.

B. Competitive Impact Analysis

As a matter of policy, the Board subjects all operational and legal changes that could have a substantial effect on payment system participants to a competitive impact analysis, even if competitive effects are not apparent on the face of the proposal.[30] Pursuant to this policy, the Board assesses whether proposed changes “would have a direct and material adverse effect on the ability of other service providers to compete effectively with the Federal Reserve in providing similar services” and whether any such adverse effect “was due to legal differences or due to a dominant market position deriving from such legal differences.” If, as a result of this analysis, the Board identifies an adverse effect on the ability to compete, the Board then assesses whether the associated benefits—such as improvements to payment system efficiency or integrity—can be achieved while minimizing the adverse effect on competition.

This final rule promulgates risk-management standards and advance notice requirements for designated FMUs, as required by Title VIII of the Act. Some FMUs may be designated on the basis of their role as operators of payment systems that compete with similar services provided by the Reserve Banks, and designation subjects the FMU to an enhanced supervisory framework.

Commenters have raised concerns regarding the Reserve Banks obtaining a competitive advantage over private-sector competitors through the Board imposing a less-stringent supervisory framework on the Reserve Banks priced services than would be imposed on a competing designated FMU. As noted above, Board oversight of the Reserve Banks goes well beyond the typical supervisory framework for private-sector entities, including the framework provided by Title VIII. The Board applies risk-management standards to the Reserve Banks' Fedwire and other financial services that are at least as stringent as those applied to designated FMUs pursuant to Title VIII. Further, the Board will hold Reserve Banks to procedural requirements that are the same as, or higher than, the requirements for designated FMUs supervised by the Board, with respect to advance notice of material changes to the rules, procedures, or operations of Reserve Bank priced services that compete with designated FMUs. Therefore, the Board does not believe the final rule promulgating risk-management standards or advance notice requirements for designated FMUs under Title VIII will have any direct and material adverse effect on the ability of other service providers to compete with the Reserve Banks.

C. Paperwork Reduction Act Analysis

In accordance with the Paperwork Reduction Act of 1995 (44 U.S.C. 3506; 5 CFR, Appendix A.1), the Board reviewed the final rule under the authority delegated to the Board by the Office of Management and Budget. As noted in the proposal, for purposes of calculating burden under the Paperwork Reduction Act, a "collection of information" involves 10 or more respondents.

Any collection of information addressed to all or a substantial majority of an industry is presumed to involve 10 or more respondents (5 CFR 1320.3(c), 1320.3(c)(4)(ii)).

The Board estimates there are fewer than 10 respondents, and these respondents do not represent all or a substantial majority of the participants in payment, clearing, and settlement systems.

Therefore, no collections of information pursuant to the Paperwork Reduction Act are contained in the final rule. The Board did not receive any comments on this analysis.

The Board has a continuing interest in the public's opinion of the collection of information.

Comments on the collection of information should be sent to Cynthia Ayouch, Acting Federal Reserve Board Clearance Officer, Division of Research and Statistics, Mail Stop 95-A, Board of Governors of the Federal Reserve System, Washington, DC 20551, with copies of such comments sent to the Office of Management and Budget, Paperwork Reduction Project (7100-0199), Washington, DC 20503.

LIST OF SUBJECTS IN 12 CFR PART 234

- Banks
- Banking
- Credit
- Electronic funds transfers
- Financial market utilities
- Securities

AUTHORITY AND ISSUANCE

For the reasons set forth in the preamble, the Board amends 12 CFR, Chapter II by adding part 234, as set forth below.

PART 234—DESIGNATED FINANCIAL MARKET UTILITIES (REGULATION HH)

- Sec.
- 234.1 Authority, purpose, and scope.
- 234.2 Definitions.
- 234.3 Standards for payment systems.
- 234.4 Standards for central securities depositories and central counterparties.
- 234.5 Changes to rules, procedures, or operations.

Authority:

12 U.S.C. 5461 *et seq.*

§ 234.1 Authority, Purpose and Scope

(a) *Authority.* This part is issued under the authority of sections 805, 806, and 810 of the Dodd-Frank Wall Street Reform and Consumer Protection Act (Dodd-Frank Act) (Pub. L. 111-203, 124 Stat. 1376; 12 U.S.C. 5464, 5465, and 5469).

(b) *Purpose and scope.* This part establishes risk-management standards governing the operations related to the payment, clearing, and settlement activities of designated financial market utilities. The risk-management standards do not apply, however, to a designated financial market utility that is a derivatives clearing organization registered under section 5b of the Commodity Exchange Act (7 U.S.C. 7a-1) or a clearing agency registered with the Securities and Exchange Commission under section 17A of the Securities Exchange Act of 1934 (15 U.S.C. 78q-1), which are governed by the risk-management standards promulgated by the Commodity Futures Trading Commission or the Securities and Exchange Commission, respectively, for which each is the Supervisory Agency (as defined below). In addition, this part sets out requirements and procedures for a designated financial market utility that proposes to make a change to its rules, procedures, or operations that could materially affect the nature or level of risks presented by the designated financial market utility and for which the Board is the Supervisory Agency.

§ 234.2 Definitions

As used in this part:

(a) *Central counterparty* means an entity that interposes itself between the counterparties to trades, acting as the buyer to every seller and the seller to every buyer.
(b) *Central securities depository* means an entity that holds securities in custody to enable securities transactions to be processed by means of book entries or an entity that enables securities to be transferred and settled by book entry either free of or against payment.
(c) *Designated financial market utility* means a financial market utility (as defined in paragraph (d) of this section) that the Financial Stability Oversight Council has designated under section 804 of the Dodd-Frank Act (12 U.S.C. 5463).
(d) *Financial market utility* has the same meaning as the term defined in section 803(6) of the Dodd-Frank Act (12 U.S.C. 5462(6)).
(e) *Payment system* means a set of payment instructions, procedures, and rules for the transfer of funds among system participants.
(f) *Supervisory Agency* has the same meaning as the term is defined in section 803(8) of the Dodd-Frank Act (12 U.S.C. 5462(8)).

§ 234.3 Standards for Payment Systems

(a) A designated financial market utility that is designated on the basis of its role as the operator of a payment system must implement rules, procedures, or operations designed to ensure that it meets or exceeds the following risk-management standards with respect to the payment, clearing, and settlement activities of that payment system:
  1) The payment system has a well-founded legal basis under all relevant jurisdictions.
  2) The payment system's rules and procedures enable participants to have a clear understanding of the payment system's impact on each of the financial risks they incur through participation in it.

3) The payment system has clearly defined procedures for the management of credit risks and liquidity risks, which specify the respective responsibilities of the payment system operator and the participants and which provide appropriate incentives to manage and contain those risks.
4) The payment system provides prompt final settlement on the day of value, during the day and at a minimum at the end of the day.
5) A payment system in which multilateral netting takes place is, at a minimum, capable of ensuring the timely completion of daily settlements in the event of an inability to settle by the participant with the largest single settlement obligation.
6) Assets used for settlement are a claim on the central bank or other assets that carry little or no credit risk and little or no liquidity risk.
7) The payment system ensures a high degree of security and operational reliability and has contingency arrangements for timely completion of daily processing.
8) The payment system provides a means of making payments that is practical for its users and efficient for the economy.
9) The payment system has objective and publicly disclosed criteria for participation, which permit fair and open access.
10) The payment system's governance arrangements are effective, accountable, and transparent.

(b) The Board, by order, may apply heightened risk-management standards to a particular designated financial market utility in accordance with the risks presented by that designated financial market utility. The Board, by order, may waive the application of a standard or standards to a particular designated financial market utility where the risks presented by or the design of that designated financial market utility would make the application of the standard or standards inappropriate.

§ 234.4 Standards for Central Securities Depositories and Central Counterparties

(a) A designated financial market utility that is designated on the basis of its role as a central securities depository or a central counterparty must implement rules, procedures, or operations designed to ensure that it meets or exceeds the following risk-management standards with respect to the payment, clearing, and settlement activities of that central securities depository or central counterparty:

1) The central securities depository or central counterparty has a well-founded, transparent, and enforceable legal framework for each aspect of its activities in all relevant jurisdictions.
2) The central securities depository or central counterparty requires participants to have sufficient financial resources and robust operational capacity to meet obligations arising from participation in the central securities depository or central counterparty. The central securities depository or central counterparty has procedures in place to monitor that participation requirements are met on an ongoing basis. The central securities depository's or central counterparty's participation requirements are objective and publicly disclosed, and permit fair and open access.
3) The central securities depository or central counterparty holds assets in a manner whereby risk of loss or of delay in its access to them is minimized. Assets invested by a central securities depository or central counterparty are held in instruments with minimal credit, market, and liquidity risks.
4) The central securities depository or central counterparty identifies sources of operational risk and minimizes them through the development of appropriate systems, controls, and procedures; has systems that are reliable and secure, and has adequate, scalable capacity; and has business continuity plans that allow for timely recovery of operations and fulfillment of the central securities depository's or central counterparty's obligations.
5) The central securities depository or central counterparty employs money settlement arrangements that eliminate or strictly limit its settlement bank risks, that is, its credit and liquidity risks from the use of banks to effect money settlements with its participants and requires funds transfers to the central securities depository or central counterparty be final when effected.
6) The central securities depository or central counterparty is cost-effective in meeting the requirements of participants while maintaining safe and secure operations.
7) The central securities depository or central counterparty evaluates the potential sources of risks that can arise when the central securities depository or central counterparty establishes links either cross-border or domestically to settle transactions or clear

trades, and ensures that the risks are managed prudently on an ongoing basis.

8) The central securities depository or central counterparty has governance arrangements that are clear and transparent to fulfill public interest requirements and to support the objectives of owners and participants and promotes the effectiveness of a central securities depository's or central counterparty's risk-management procedures.
9) The central securities depository or central counterparty provides market participants with sufficient information for them to identify and evaluate accurately the risks and costs associated with using its services.
10) The central securities depository or central counterparty establishes default procedures that ensures that the central securities depository or central counterparty can take timely action to contain losses and liquidity pressures and to continue meeting its obligations and provides for key aspects of the default procedures to be publicly available.
11) The central securities depository or central counterparty ensures that final settlement occurs no later than the end of the settlement day and requires that intraday or real-time finality be provided where necessary to reduce risks.
12) The central securities depository or central counterparty eliminates principal risk by linking securities transfers to funds transfers in a way that achieves delivery versus payment.
13) The central securities depository or central counterparty states its obligations with respect to physical deliveries, and the risks from these obligations are identified and managed.
14) The central securities depository immobilizes or dematerializes securities certificates and transfers them by book entry to the greatest extent possible.
15) The central securities depository institutes risk controls that include collateral requirements and limits, and ensure timely settlement in the event that the participant with the largest payment obligation is unable to settle when the central securities depository extends intraday credit.
16) The central counterparty measures its credit exposures to its participants at least once a day and limits its exposures to potential losses from defaults by its participants in normal market

conditions so that the operations of the central counterparty would not be disrupted and non-defaulting participants would not be exposed to losses that they cannot anticipate or control.

17) The central counterparty uses margin requirements to limit its credit exposures to participants in normal market conditions and uses risk-based models and parameters to set margin requirements and reviews them regularly. Specifically, the centralcounter-party—

i. Provides for annual model validation consisting of evaluating the performance of the central counterparty's margin models and the related parameters and assumptions associated with such models by a qualified person who does not perform functions associated with the central counterparty's margin models (except as part of the annual model validation) and does not report to such a person.

ii. Reviews and backtests margin models and parameters at least quarterly.

18) The central counterparty maintains sufficient financial resources to withstand, at a minimum, a default by the participant to which it has the largest exposure in extreme but plausible market conditions.

(b) The Board, by order, may apply heightened risk-management standards to a particular designated financial market utility in accordance with the risks presented by that designated financial market utility. The Board, by order, may waive the application of a standard or standards to a particular designated financial market utility where the risks presented by or the design of that designated financial market utility would make the application of the standard or standards inappropriate.

§ 234.5 Changes to Rules, Procedures, or Operations

(a) *Advance notice.*

1) A designated financial market utility shall provide at least 60-days advance notice to the Board of any proposed change to its rules, procedures, or operations that could materially affect the nature or level of risks presented by the designated financial market utility.

2) The notice of the proposed change shall describe—

i. The nature of the change and expected effects on risks to the designated financial market utility, its participants, or the market; and

ii. How the designated financial market utility plans to manage any identified risks.

3) The Board may require the designated financial market utility to provide additional information necessary to assess the effect the proposed change would have on the nature or level of risks associated with the utility's payment, clearing, or settlement activities and the sufficiency of any proposed risk-management techniques.

4) A designated financial market utility shall not implement a change to which the Board has an objection.

5) (The Board will notify the designated financial market utility of any objection before the end of 60 days after the later of—

i. The date the Board receives the notice of proposed change; or

ii. The date the Board receives any further information it requests for consideration of the notice.

6) A designated financial market utility may implement a change if it has not received an objection to the proposed change before the end of 60 days after the later of—

i. The date the Board receives the notice of proposed change; or

ii. The date the Board receives any further information it requests for consideration of the notice.

7) (7) With respect to proposed changes that raise novel or complex issues, the Board may, by written notice during the 60-day review period, extend the review period for an additional 60 days. Any extension under this paragraph will extend the time periods under paragraphs (a)(5) and (a)(6) of this section to 120 days.

8) (8) A designated financial market utility may implement a proposed change before the expiration of the applicable review period if the Board notifies the designated financial market utility in writing that the Board does not object to the proposed change and authorizes the designated financial market utility to implement the change on an earlier date, subject to any conditions imposed by the Board.

(b) *Emergency changes.*

1) A designated financial market utility may implement a change that would otherwise require advance notice under this section if it determines that—
   i. An emergency exists; and
   ii. Immediate implementation of the change is necessary for the designated financial market utility to continue to provide its services in a safe and sound manner.
2) The designated financial market utility shall provide notice of any such emergency change to the Board as soon as practicable and no later than 24 hours after implementation of the change.
3) In addition to the information required for changes requiring advance notice in paragraph (a)(2) of this section, the notice of an emergency change shall describe—
   i. The nature of the emergency; and
   ii. The reason the change was necessary for the designated financial market utility to continue to provide its services in a safe and sound manner.
4) The Board may require modification or rescission of the change if it finds that the change is not consistent with the purposes of the Dodd-Frank Act or any applicable rules, order, or standards prescribed under section 805(a) of the Dodd-Frank Act.

(c) *Materiality.*

1) The term "materially affect the nature or level of risks presented" in paragraph (a)(1) of this section means matters as to which there is a reasonable possibility that the change would materially affect the overall nature or level of risk presented by the designated financial market utility, including risk arising in the performance of payment, clearing, or settlement functions.
2) A change to rules, procedures, or operations that would materially affect the nature or level of risks presented includes, but is not limited to, changes that materially affect any one or more of the following:
   i. Participant eligibility or access criteria;
   ii. Product eligibility;
   iii. Risk management;
   iv. Settlement failure or default procedures;
   v. Financial resources;
   vi. Business continuity and disaster recovery plans;
   vii. Daily or intraday settlement procedures;

viii. The scope of services, including the addition of a new service or discontinuation of an existing service;

ix. Technical design or operating platform, which results in non-routine changes to the underlying technological framework for payment, clearing, or settlement functions; or

x. Governance.

3) A change to rules, procedures, or operations that does not meet the conditions of paragraph (c)(2) of this section and would not materially affect the nature or level of risks presented includes, but is not limited to the following:

i. A routine technology systems upgrade;

ii. A change in a fee, price, or other charge for services provided by the designated financial market utility;

iii. A change related solely to the administration of the designated financial market utility or related to the routine, daily administration, direction, and control of employees; or

iv. A clerical change and other non-substantive revisions to rules, procedures, or other documentation.

By order of the Board of Governors of the Federal Reserve System, July 27, 2012.

Robert deV. Frierson,

Deputy Secretary of the Board.

[FR Doc. 2012-18762 Filed 8-1-12; 8:45 am]

BILLING CODE P

End Notes

[1]. The Dodd-Frank Act, Public Law 111-203, 124 Stat. 1376, was signed into law on July 21, 2010.

[2]. Under section 805(a)(2) of the Act, the CFTC and the SEC are also required to take relevant international standards and existing prudential requirements into consideration in prescribing regulations containing risk-management standards governing designated clearing entities.

[3]. A Supervisory Agency includes the SEC and CFTC with respect to their respective designated clearing entities (as defined above), the appropriate federal banking agencies (including the Board) with respect to FMUs that are institutions described in section 3(q) of the Federal Deposit Insurance Act (12 U.S.C. 1813(q)), and the Board with respect to a designated FMU that is otherwise not subject to the jurisdiction of any of the agencies listed above.

[4]. See 76 FR 18445 (Apr. 4, 2011).

[5]. In addition, the Board is adopting several changes intended to clarify the requirements of the regulation.

[6]. See 76 FR at 18447.

[7]. The PSR policy is available on the Board's public Web site at: *http://www.federalreserve.gov/paymentsystems/psr_policy.htm.*

[8]. The *Principles for Financial Market Infrastructures* are available at *http://www.bis.org/publ/cpss101a.pdf.* The final report reflects comments received during the public consultation period from March 10, 2011 to July 29, 2011.

[9]. See 76 FR 44763, 44769 (July 27, 2011).

[10]. See 76 FR at 44769. The Council also decided, however, against including in the final rule any categorical exclusion for FMUs operating retail payment or other systems, both because there are not clear distinctions between various types of systems, and because such an exclusion would impair the Council's ability to respond appropriately to new information, changed circumstances, and future developments.

[11]. To conform to these modifications, the Board is revising the definitions in § 234.2 (a), (b), and (e).

[12]. One commenter raised similar concerns with the corresponding access criteria and governance standards in proposed § 234.4(a)(2) and (8) with respect to CSDs and CCPs.

[13]. For example, a designated FMU may set access criteria based on risk measures such as capital ratios, risk ratings, or other indicators.

[14]. Proposed § 234.4(a)(17)(i) inadvertently referred to the margin models of the "clearing agency." The Board has revised these references to "central counterparty" in the final rule.

[15]. This position is generally consistent with current supervisory guidance on model risk management by banks. See SR letter 11-7, p.3 (Apr. 4, 2011), which states: Validation involves a degree of independence from model development and use. Generally, validation is done by staff who are not responsible for model development or use and do not have a stake in whether a model is determined to be valid.As a practical matter, some validation work may be most effectively done by model developers and users; it is essential, however, that such validation work be subject to critical review by an independent party, who should conduct additional activities to ensure proper validation. Overall, the quality of the validation process is indicated by critical review by objective, knowledgeable parties and the actions taken to address issues identified by those parties.

[16]. On November 8, 2011, pursuant to its authority under Title VII of the Dodd-Frank Act, the CFTC published its final rule on risk-management standards for DCOs. The CFTC elected to adopt a cover one requirement for all DCOs, and delay risk-management related rulemakings for systemically important DCOs until a later time. See 76 FR 69334 (Nov. 8, 2011).

[17]. *See*§ 234.4(b).

[18]. 76 FR at 18447.

[19]. The Core Principles and the Recommendations for Securities Settlement Systems were incorporated into the PSR policy in 2004 (*http://www.federalreserve.gov/boarddocs/press/other/2004/20041126/default.htm*). The Recommendations for Central Counterparties was incorporated into the PSR policy in 2007 (*http://www.federalreserve. gov/newsevents/press/other/20070112a.htm*).

[20]. One example of this approach is the financial resource coverage standard in § 234.4(a)(15) and (18) (cover one versus cover two).

[21]. "Could" is commonly defined as the past tense of "can," and is used to indicate "possibility." "Likely" is defined as "possessing or displaying the qualities or characteristics that make

something probable." American Heritage Dictionary of the English Language (Fourth Edition), *http://ahdictionary.com/.*

[22]. The risks presented by the designated FMU's performance of its PCS functions can go beyond the effect on the designated FMU itself and reach its participants or the market more broadly.

[23]. One commenter suggested that the final rule include in the non-material list of proposed § 234.5(c)(3) a greater range of operating rule changes for designated FMUs participating in the retail payment systems. As explained above, however, the Council has indicated that it expects to focus at this time on FMUs that operate large-value systems and not on FMUs that operate low-value systems, such as check or ACH. 76 FR 44763, 44769 (July 2011).

[24]. 12 U.S.C. 221 *et seq.*

[25]. See the Board's policy on "Oversight of Key Financial Infrastructures" related to Reserve Bank Systems at *http://www.federalreserve.gov/paymentsystems/over_rbsystems.htm.*

[26]. 12 U.S.C. 248a. These costs are included in the private-sector adjustment factor for pricing Reserve Bank priced services.

[27]. 12 U.S.C. 248a(c)(3).

[28]. The Board policy can be found at: *http://www.federalreserve.gov/paymentsystems/pfs_standards.htm.*

[29]. See footnote 19.

[30]. See "The Federal Reserve in the Payments System," Fed. Res. Reg. Svc. § 9-1550, 9-1558 (Apr. 2009).

For further information contact:

Jennifer A. Lucier, Assistant Director (202) 872-7581 or Kathy C. Wang, Senior Financial Services Analyst (202) 872-4991, Division of Reserve Bank Operations and Payment Systems; Christopher W. Clubb, Senior Counsel (202) 452-3904 or Kara L. Handzlik, Senior Attorney (202) 452-3852, Legal Division; for users of Telecommunications Device for the Deaf (TDD) only, contact (202) 263-4869.

URL to this document is https://federalregister.gov/a/2012-18762

In: Financial Market Utilities …
Editor: Jovan Barank

ISBN: 978-1-62618-052-9

Chapter 3

THE DODD-FRANK WALL STREET REFORM AND CONSUMER PROTECTION ACT: TITLE VII, DERIVATIVES*

Rena S. Miller and Kathleen Ann Ruane

SUMMARY

The financial crisis implicated the over-the-counter (OTC) derivatives market as a major source of systemic risk. A number of firms used derivatives to construct highly leveraged speculative positions, which generated enormous losses that threatened to bankrupt not only the firms themselves but also their creditors and trading partners. Hundreds of billions of dollars in government credit were needed to prevent such losses from cascading throughout the system. AIG was the best-known example, but by no means the only one.

Equally troublesome was the fact that the OTC market depended on the financial stability of a dozen or so major dealers. Failure of a dealer would have resulted in the nullification of trillions of dollars worth of contracts and would have exposed derivatives counterparties to sudden risk and loss, exacerbating the cycle of deleveraging and withholding of credit that characterized the crisis. During the crisis, all the major dealers came under stress, and even though derivatives dealing was not generally

* This is an edited, reformatted and augmented version of a Congressional Research Service publication, CRS Report for Congress R41398, prepared for Members and Committees of Congress, from www.crs.gov, dated November 6, 2012.

the direct source of financial weakness, a collapse of the $600 trillion OTC derivatives market was imminent absent federal intervention. The first group of Troubled Asset Relief Program (TARP) recipients included nearly all the large derivatives dealers.

The Dodd-Frank Act (P.L. 111-203) sought to remake the OTC market in the image of the regulated futures exchanges. Crucial reforms include a requirement that swap contracts be cleared through a central counterparty regulated by one or more federal agencies. Clearinghouses require traders to put down cash (called initial margin) at the time they open a contract to cover potential losses, and require subsequent deposits (called maintenance margin) to cover actual losses to the position. The intended effect of margin requirements is to eliminate the possibility that any firm can build up an uncapitalized exposure so large that default would have systemic consequences (again, the AIG situation). The size of a cleared position is limited by the firm's ability to post capital to cover its losses. That capital protects its trading partners and the system as a whole.

Swap dealers and major swap participants—firms with substantial derivatives positions—will be subject to margin and capital requirements above and beyond what the clearinghouses mandate. Swaps that are cleared will also be subject to trading on an exchange, or an exchange-like "swap execution facility," regulated by either the Commodity Futures Trading Commission (CFTC) or the Securities and Exchange Commission (SEC), in the case of security-based swaps. All trades will be reported to data repositories, so that regulators will have complete information about all derivatives positions. Data on swap prices and trading volumes will be made public.

The Dodd-Frank Act provides exceptions to the clearing and trading requirements for commercial end-users, or firms that use derivatives to hedge the risks of their nonfinancial business operations. Regulators may also provide exemptions for smaller financial institutions. Even trades that are exempt from the clearing and exchange-trading requirements, however, will have to be reported to data repositories or directly to regulators.

This report describes some of the requirements placed on the derivatives market by the Dodd-Frank Act.

INTRODUCTION

Prior to the financial crisis that began in 2007, over-the-counter (OTC) derivatives were generally regarded as a beneficial financial innovation that distributed financial risk more efficiently and made the financial system more stable, resilient, and resistant to shocks. The crisis essentially reversed this view. The Dodd-Frank Act (P.L. 111-203) attempts to address the aspect of the OTC market that appeared most troublesome in the crisis: the market permitted enormous exposure to risk to grow out of the sight of regulators and other traders. Derivatives exposures that could not be readily quantified exacerbated panic and uncertainty about the true financial condition of other market participants, contributing to the freezing of credit markets. Under Dodd-Frank, risk exposures of major financial institutions must be backed by capital, minimizing the shock to the financial system should such a firm fail. In addition, regulators will have information about the size and distribution of possible losses during periods of market volatility.

BACKGROUND

Derivative contracts are an array of financial instruments with one feature in common: their value is linked to changes in some underlying variable, such as the price of a physical commodity, a stock index, or an interest rate. Derivatives contracts—futures contracts, options, and swaps[1]— gain or lose value as the underlying rates or prices change, even though the holder may not actually own the underlying asset.

Thousands of firms use derivatives to manage risk. For example, a firm can protect itself against increases in the price of a commodity that it uses in production by entering into a derivative contract that will gain value if the price of the commodity rises. A notable instance of this type of hedging strategy was Southwest Airlines' derivatives position that allowed it to buy jet fuel at a low fixed price in 2008 when energy prices reached record highs. When used to hedge risk, derivatives can protect businesses (and sometimes their customers as well) from unfavorable price shocks.

Others use derivatives to seek profits by betting on which way prices will move. Such speculators provide liquidity to the market—they assume the risks that hedgers wish to avoid. The combined trading activity of hedgers and speculators provides another public benefit: price discovery. By incorporating all known information and expectations about future prices, derivatives markets generate prices that often serve as a reference point for transactions in the underlying cash markets.

Although derivatives trading had its origins in agriculture, today most derivatives are linked to financial variables, such as interest rates, foreign exchange, stock prices and indices, and the creditworthiness of issuers of bonds. The market is measured in the hundreds of trillions of dollars, and billions of contracts are traded annually.

Derivatives have also played a part in the development of complex financial instruments, such as bonds backed by pools of other assets. They can be used to create "synthetic" securities—contracts structured to replicate the returns on individual securities or portfolios of stocks, bonds, or other derivatives. Although the basic concepts of derivative finance are neither new nor particularly difficult, much of the most sophisticated financial engineering of the past few decades has involved the construction of increasingly complex mathematical models of how markets move and how different financial variables interact. Derivatives trading is often a primary path through which such research reaches the marketplace.

Since 2000, growth in derivatives markets has been explosive (although the financial crisis has caused some retrenchment since 2008). Between 2000 and the end of 2008, the volume of derivatives contracts traded on exchanges,[2] such as futures exchanges, and the notional value of total contracts traded in the over-the-counter (OTC) market[3] grew by 475% and 522%, respectively. By contrast, during the credit and housing booms that occurred over the same period, the value of corporate bonds and home mortgage debt outstanding grew by only 95% and 115%, respectively.[4] Following the 2008 financial crisis, the total notional value of OTC derivatives globally fell about 13%, but then crept upward again.[5] Total notional values outstanding for OTC derivatives globally fell from $684 trillion as of June 2008, to $592 trillion in December 2008, and then rose again to $648 trillion as of December, 2011.[6]

Pre-Dodd-Frank Act Market Structure and Regulation

The various types of derivatives are used for the same purposes—avoiding business risk, or hedging, and taking on risk in search of speculative profits. Prior to the Dodd-Frank Act, however, the instruments were traded on different types of markets. Futures contracts are traded on exchanges regulated by the Commodity Futures Trading Commission (CFTC); stock options on exchanges under the Securities and Exchange Commission (SEC); and all swaps (and security-based swaps, as well as some options) were traded over-the-counter, and were not regulated by anyone.

Exchanges are centralized markets where all the buying and selling interest comes together. Traders who want to buy (or take a long position) interact with those who want to sell (or go short), and deals are made and prices reported throughout the day. In the OTC market, contracts are made bilaterally, typically between a dealer and an end user, and there was generally no requirement that the price, the terms, or even the existence of the contract be disclosed to a regulator or to the public.

Derivatives can be volatile contracts, and the normal expectation is that there will be big gains and losses among traders. As a result, there is an issue of market integrity. How do the longs know that the shorts will be able to meet their obligations, and vice versa?

A market where billions of contracts change hands is impossible if all traders must investigate the creditworthiness of the other trader, or counterparty. The exchange market deals with this credit risk problem in one way, the OTC market in another way. How this risk—often called counterparty risk—must be managed was a key element of the reforms implemented by the Dodd-Frank Act.

Market Structure for Cleared and Exchange-Traded Derivatives

The exchanges deal with the issue of credit risk with a clearinghouse.[7] The process is shown in *Figure 1* below. (1) Two traders agree on a transaction on the exchange floor or on an electronic platform. (2) Once the trade is made, it goes to the clearinghouse, which guarantees payment to both parties. (3) In effect, the original contract between long and short traders is now two contracts, one between each trader and the clearinghouse. Traders then do not have to worry about counterparty default because the clearinghouse stands behind all trades.

But the credit risk remains: how does the clearinghouse ensure that it can meet its obligations? Clearing depends on a system of margin, or collateral. Before the trade, both the long and short traders have to deposit an initial margin payment with the clearinghouse to cover potential losses. Then at the end of each trading day, all contracts are repriced, or "marked to market," and all those who have lost money (because prices moved against them) must post additional margin (called variation or maintenance margin) to cover those losses before the next trading session.

This is known as a margin call: traders must make good on their losses immediately, or their broker may close out their positions when trading opens the next day.

The effect of the margin system is that no one can build up a large paper loss that could damage the clearinghouse in case of default: it is certainly possible to lose large amounts of money trading on the futures exchanges, but only on a "pay as you go" basis.

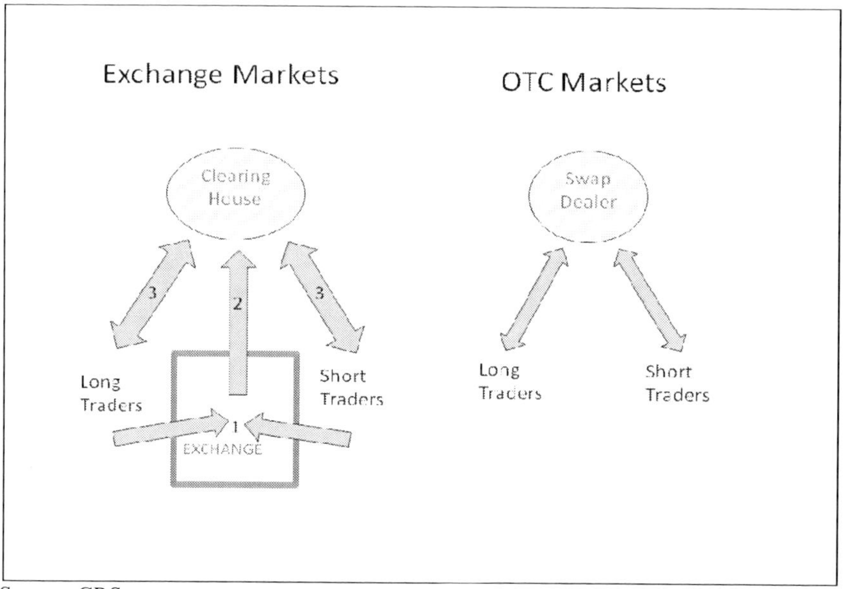

Source: CRS.

Figure 1. Pre-Dodd-Frank Act Derivatives Market Structures: Exchange and Over-the-Counter. (OTC)

Market Structure for OTC Derivatives

In the OTC market, as shown on the right side of *Figure 1*, the long and short traders do not interact directly. Instead of a centralized marketplace, there is a network of dealers who stand ready to take either long or short positions, and make money on spreads and fees. The dealer absorbs the credit risk of customer default, while the customer faces the risk of dealer default. In this kind of market, one would expect the dealers to be the most solid and creditworthy financial institutions, and in fact the OTC market that emerged has been dominated by a dozen or so firms—very large institutions like JP Morgan Chase, Goldman Sachs, Citigroup, Bank of America, Morgan Stanley and their foreign counterparts. Before 2007, such firms were generally viewed as too well diversified or too well managed to fail; in 2008, their fallibility was well established, and a pertinent question now is whether the government would still consider them to be too big to fail. (Title II of Dodd-Frank seeks to ensure that it will not.[8]) In the OTC market, some contracts required collateral or margin, but not all. There was no standard practice: all contract terms were negotiable. A trade group, the International Swaps and Derivatives Association (ISDA), published best practice standards for use of collateral, but compliance was voluntary. Because there was no universal, mandatory system of margin, large uncollateralized losses could (and did) build up in the OTC market. Perhaps the best-known example in the crisis was AIG, which wrote about $1.8 trillion worth of credit default swaps guaranteeing payment if certain mortgage-backed securities defaulted or experienced other "credit events."[9] Many of AIG's contracts required it to post collateral as the credit quality of the underlying referenced securities (or AIG's own credit rating) deteriorated, but AIG did not post initial margin, as this was deemed unnecessary because of the firm's triple-A rating. As the subprime crisis worsened, AIG faced margin calls that it could not meet. To avert bankruptcy, with the risk of global financial chaos, the Federal Reserve and the Treasury put tens of billions of dollars into AIG, the bulk of which went to its derivatives counterparties.[10]

A key reform in Dodd-Frank is a mandate that many OTC swaps be cleared, which means that they will be subject to margin requirements. This will have the effect of combining features of the two market structures shown in *Figure 1*.

THE DODD-FRANK ACT'S CLEARING AND REPORTING REQUIREMENTS

The Dodd-Frank Act requires that most derivatives contracts formerly traded exclusively in the OTC market be cleared and traded on exchanges. Traders in these products now are required to post margin in the fashion described above and have their contracts repriced at the close of each trading day. It is important to note that not all derivatives contracts are required to be traded in this way by the act. The Dodd-Frank Act presumes that some derivatives contracts will still be traded in the OTC market; however, it grants regulators broader powers to obtain information about these derivatives and impose margin and capital requirements on them as well. The CFTC and the SEC have been working to issue regulations that implement these provisions.

Clearing Requirement

Title VII of the Dodd-Frank Act creates largely parallel clearing and exchange trading requirements for swaps and security-based swaps as those terms are defined by Title VII and further clarified by the CFTC and the SEC in a joint rulemaking.[11] Section 723 creates the clearing and exchange trading requirements for swaps over which the CFTC has jurisdiction.[12] Section 763 creates largely parallel requirements for security-based swaps over which the SEC has authority.[13]

If a swap or security-based swap is required to be cleared, the Dodd-Frank Act makes it unlawful for parties to enter into swaps or security-based swaps unless the transaction has been submitted for clearing.[14] There are two ways in which a swap or security-based swap may become subject to the clearing requirement.[15] In the first way, the agency of jurisdiction is required to engage in an ongoing review of the products it has jurisdiction over to determine whether a particular swap, security-based swap, group, or class of such contracts should be subject to the clearing requirement. Determinations made on the initiative of the commissions are discussed further in the "Prevention of Evasion" section below.

The second way in which a swap or security-based swap may become subject to the clearing requirement under the Dodd-Frank Act is upon submission to the CFTC or the SEC. In the joint rules issued by the CFTC and SEC further defining swaps and security-based swaps, any person may submit a request to the CFTC or the SEC for a public interpretation of whether an instrument is covered by this title.[16] Furthermore, when a derivatives clearing organization[17] (swaps) or clearing agency[18] (security-based swaps) decides to accept a swap or security-based swap for clearing, the act requires the organization to submit the transactions to the relevant commission for a determination as to whether the transactions should be required to be cleared. Furthermore, upon enactment of the Dodd-Frank Act, all swaps and security-based swaps that were listed for clearing by derivatives clearing organizations and clearing agencies at the time of passage were deemed submitted to the SEC and the CFTC for a determination of whether the clearing requirement should apply.

Following submission to the agencies, the agencies have 90 days to determine whether the swaps or security-based swaps are subject to the clearing requirement, unless the submitting organization agrees to an extension. When making that determination, the agencies must consider (1) "the existence of significant outstanding notional exposures, trading liquidity, and adequate pricing data"; (2) "the availability of rule framework, capacity, operational expertise and resources, and credit support infrastructure to clear the contract on terms consistent with material terms and trading conventions on which the contract is then traded"; (3) "the effect on the mitigation of systemic risk ..."; (4) "the effect on competition, including appropriate fees and charges ..."; and (5) "the existence of reasonable legal certainty in the event of the insolvency of the relevant derivatives clearing organization or 1 or more of its clearing members with regard to the treatment of customer and swap counterparty positions, funds, and property."[19] In the process of making these determinations, the agencies are also required to allow the public to comment on whether the clearing requirement should apply.

Should the CFTC or the SEC determine that a particular swap or security-based swap is required to be cleared, counterparties to that type of transaction may apply to stay the clearing requirement until the relevant agency "completes a review of the terms" of the swap or security-based swap and the clearing requirement.[20] Under the act, upon completing the review, the relevant agency may require the swap or security-based swap to be cleared, either unconditionally or subject to appropriate conditions. The relevant agency may also determine that the swap or security-based swap is not required to be cleared.

With certain exceptions, for example if one of the counterparties qualifies for the end-user exemption, counterparties to swaps and security-based swaps that are required to be cleared must either execute the transactions on exchanges or specialized execution facilities.[21]

As of this writing, the clearing requirement for swaps has yet to take effect. The CFTC is in the process of implementing the clearing requirement for many derivatives contracts. Rules were proposed in August and the initial comment period closed in September of 2012.[22] The SEC has issued final rules for the mandatory clearing of security-based swaps.[23]

The Exchange-Trading Requirement

With certain exceptions, swaps and security-based swaps that are required to be cleared must also be executed on a regulated exchange or on a trading platform defined in the act as a swaps execution facility (SEF) or a security-based swaps execution facility (SBSEF). Such facilities must permit multiple market participants to trade by accepting bids or offers made by multiple participants in the facility.

The goal of the trading requirement is "to promote pre-trade price transparency in the swaps market."[24] Because the old OTC market was notably opaque, with complete price information available only to dealers, swaps customers were limited in their ability to shop for the best price or rate. The expectation is that as price information becomes more widely available, competition will produce narrower spreads by lowering prices.

SEFs and SBSEFs must comply with a number of core principles set out in the act. While these are somewhat less prescriptive than the regulation of exchanges where public customers are allowed to trade,[25] the new trading facilities have regulatory and administrative responsibilities far beyond what applied to OTC trading desks in the past. Among other things, SEFs and SBSEFs must

- establish and enforce rules to prevent trading abuses and to provide impartial access to the trading facility;
- ensure that swap contracts are not readily susceptible to manipulation;
- monitor trading to prevent manipulation, price distortion, and disruptions in the underlying cash market;
- set position limits;
- maintain adequate financial and managerial resources, including safeguards against operational risk;
- maintain an audit trail of all transactions;
- publish timely data on prices and trading volume;
- adopt emergency rules governing liquidation or transfer of trading positions as well as trading halts; and
- employ a chief compliance officer, who will submit an annual report to regulators.

During consideration of Dodd-Frank, a central issue of debate was the extent to which existing OTC derivatives trading platforms and mechanisms could be accommodated under the new regulatory regime. OTC trading practices ranged from individual telephone negotiations to electronic systems accessible to multiple participants. One concern was that if SEFs were too much like exchanges, the existing futures and securities exchanges would monopolize trading. On the other hand, if the SEF definition were too vague or general, the OTC market might remain opaque.

The bill reported by the Senate Banking Committee defined SEF as "an electronic trading system with pre-trade and post-trade transparency."[26] The explicit reference to "pre-trade" transparency does not appear in the final legislation, in part because of concerns that such a requirement was not compatible with the business models of a number of intermediaries, such as interdealer swap brokers providing anonymous execution services.[27]

As is the case with the clearing requirement, Dodd-Frank provides exceptions to the exchange-trading mandate. If no exchange or SEF or SBSEF makes a swap available for trading, the contract may be traded OTC. A swap that meets the end-user clearing exemption is likewise exempt from the exchange trading requirement. We discuss the end-user exemption in more detail in the next section.

The CFTC issued a proposed rule, on January 7, 2011, that would further define certain minimum requirements for swap execution facilities.[28] The proposed definition of SEF is parallel to the existing Commodity Exchange Act definition of "trading facility"—a platform where multiple participants have the capacity to post bids and offers to all other parties participating in the facility. The rules would exclude "one-to-one" systems such as telephone voice brokers, and "one-to-many" platforms such as single-dealer trading facilities. Such systems, in the CFTC's view, are not compatible with impartial access requirements of the statute.[29]

SEFs will provide pre-trade price transparency—the ability for all market participants to see quoted prices before transacting—for (1) trades that must be cleared; (2) for all swaps that are made available for trading on a SEF; and (3) trades that are below the size of a block trade. Pre-trade transparency requirements will not apply to (1) block trades, (2) end-user trades, or (3) contracts that are not available for trading on a SEF. Price data will be made public according to the rules on real-time reporting discussed above.

The SEC issued a proposed rule on security-based swap execution facilities on February 2, 2011.[30] The rule appears to be generally similar to the CFTC's SEF proposal. The principal requirement for a security-based SEF is that it be a system or platform that allows more than one participant to interact with the trading interest of more than one other participant on the system or platform.

End-User Exemption

Sections 723 and 763 of the Dodd-Frank Act provide exceptions to the clearing requirement for swaps and security-based swaps when one of the counterparties to the transaction is not a financial entity; is using the transaction to hedge or mitigate its own commercial risk; and notifies the relevant agency "how it generally meets its financial obligations associated with entering into non-cleared swaps."[31] This has been widely referred to as the end-user exemption because it applies only to transactions where at least one counterparty is "not a financial entity."[32]

A financial entity for the purposes of this section is defined as a swap dealer, a security-based swap dealer, a major swap participant (MSP), a major security-based swap participant, a commodity pool, a private fund, an employee benefit plan, or a person predominantly engaged in activities that are in the business of banking, or in activities that are financial in nature.[33] To illustrate, a prime example of an entity that would not be a financial entity, but that may engage in swaps trading as a necessary part of the entity's business, would be an airline that regularly trades in fuel derivatives to offset potential volatility in the market for jet fuel.[34] Under the act, eligible counterparties may also use an affiliate ("including affiliate entities predominantly engaged in providing financing for the purchase of the merchandise or manufactured goods of the person") to engage in swaps or security-based swaps under the condition that the affiliate "act on behalf of the person [qualifying for the exemption] and as an agent, uses the swap to hedge or mitigate the commercial risk of the person or other affiliate of the person that is not a financial entity."[35] Financial entities wholly controlled by the end-user and whose primary business is hedging the commercial risk of the end user may also qualify for the end-user exemption. Finally, the act allows regulators to exclude depository institutions, farm credit institutions, and credit unions with $10 billion or less in assets from the definition of "financial entity," allowing small financial entities (e.g., small banks) to qualify for the end-user exemption as well.[36]

In order to qualify for the exemption from the clearing requirement, it is not enough to be a nonfinancial entity (or, in some circumstances a financial entity that qualifies for the exemption, nonetheless). The swaps engaged in by the entity must be for the purpose of hedging or mitigating commercial risk. According to the CFTC's final rule defining the end-user exemption, an entity will be engaging in a swap to hedge or mitigate its own commercial risk under the following circumstances. First, the swap must meet one of the following three criteria. It must be economically appropriate to the reduction of risks conducted by the company; it must qualify as a bona fide hedge for purposes of being exempt from position limits under the CEA; or, it must qualify for hedging treatment under Financial Accounting Standards Board Accounting Standards Codification Topic 815, Derivatives and Hedging (formerly known as Statement No. 133) or Governmental Accounting Standards Board Statement 53, Accounting and Financial Reporting for Derivative Instruments. Second, the swap must not be used either for "a purpose that is in the nature of speculation, investing or trading," or "to hedge or mitigate the risk of another swap or security-based swap position, unless that other position itself is used to hedge or mitigate commercial risk."[37]

The application of the clearing exemption provided by Sections 723 and 763 of the Dodd-Frank Act is at the discretion of the counterparty that qualifies for the exemption. Eligible counterparties may elect to clear the transaction, and may choose which derivatives clearing organization or clearing agency shall clear the transaction. If the eligible counterparty chooses to use the end-user exemption, however, the counterparty must disclose the transaction to the relevant regulator and inform the regulator "how it generally meets its financial obligations associated with entering into non-cleared swaps."[38] It is also important to note that this exemption applies on a swap by swap basis. As a result, even though a non-financial entity can use the exemption for swaps in which it engages that are related to legitimate hedging activities, if other swaps to which the non-financial entity is a party do not meet the requirements for the definition of a legitimate hedge, laid out by the CFTC, those swaps will be required to be cleared.

The CFTC rules implementing this exemption were issued in September of 2012. However, the rules will not officially apply until the clearing requirement takes effect. As noted above, the CFTC has not yet issued final rules implementing the clearing requirement.

The SEC has proposed rules to implement the end-user exemption for security-based swaps.[39] The rules have yet to become final.

Major Swap Participant and Swap Dealer Definitions

A basic theme in Dodd-Frank is that systemically important financial institutions should maintain capital cushions above and beyond what specific regulations require in order to compensate for the risk that their failure would pose to the financial system and the economy. In addition to the margin requirements that apply to individual derivatives contracts, major participants in derivatives markets will become subject to prudential regulation in Title VII. Two categories of regulated market participants are enumerated: swap dealers and major swap participants (together with the security-based swap equivalents).

Since the OTC dealer market is highly concentrated, the proposal that swap dealers be subject to additional prudential regulation was not controversial. Only a few dozen of the largest financial institutions were presumed to be affected. The question of how many firms should be included in the definition of major swap participant (MSP), however, was contentious. How many non-dealer and non-bank firms should become subject to prudential regulation?

Several MSP definitions were considered in the House; the version of H.R. 4173 that passed the House in December 2009 defined an MSP as a non-dealer holding a "substantial net position" in swaps, excluding positions held to hedge commercial risk, or whose counterparties would suffer "significant credit losses" in the event of an MSP default.[40] Neither "substantial net position," "significant loss," nor "commercial risk" was defined in the bill. However, the bill provided guidance to regulators: the first two terms were linked to "systemically important entities" that can "significantly impact the financial system through counterparty credit risk."

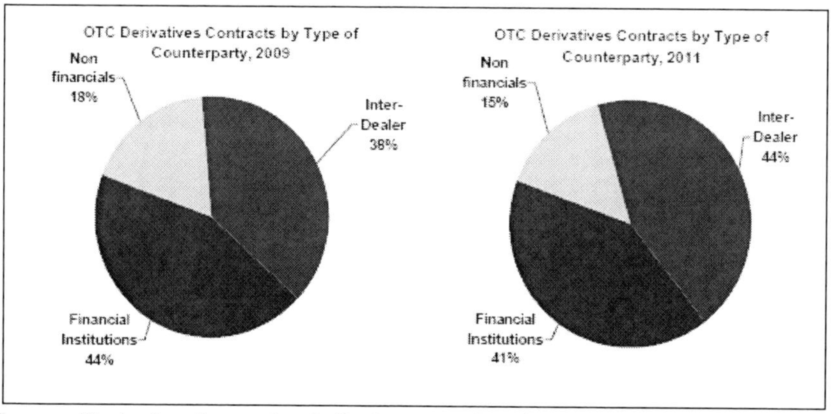

Source: Bank for International Settlements, Regular OTC Derivatives Market Statistics, May 2010 and May 2012.

Notes: Includes interest rate, foreign exchange, equity, and credit default swaps. Because this chart describes the global market, which may fall outside United States jurisdiction, some contracts covered by the chart will not be covered by Dodd-Frank regulations.

Figure 2. Global OTC Derivatives Contracts by Type of Counterparty: 2009 and 2011.

The MSP definition in the bill that passed the House in December 2009 sought to prevent regulators from defining the key terms ("substantial position, "significant loss," etc.) in a way that imposed prudential regulation on most firms that used derivatives to hedge risk. In addition, MSPs were required to clear their swap contracts, and the cost of clearing was regarded as burdensome for end-users. Under the House definition, it seemed plausible that relatively few firms would be defined as MSPs—Fannie Mae and Freddie Mac, a few large non-dealer banks and insurance companies, and perhaps a few large hedge funds.

There was an opposite concern: that if the end-user exemption were too broad, and the MSP definition too narrow, significant volumes of OTC trading might escape the new regulatory scheme. Error! Reference source not found. above suggests that if mandatory clearing were applied only to inter-dealer trades in 2009, nearly two-thirds of the market would be unaffected. Nearly half the OTC contracts in 2009 were between a dealer and another financial institution: how many of these would be covered? While only 18% of transactions in 2009 involved nonfinancial counterparties, was it possible that risky trading activities could migrate from banks to nonfinancial firms if the exemption for hedging commercial risk were not in some way circumscribed?

Two versions of the MSP definition were considered in the Senate. The Banking Committee approved S. 3217 on April 15, 2010, including an MSP definition without the references to systemic importance that appeared in the House bill.[41] In other words, the regulators were given wide discretion to designate as MSPs firms that were not systemically important. The Senate Agriculture Committee produced another MSP definition, which was included in the bill that passed the Senate. It included "systemically significant" language generally similar to the House's, but added new prongs to the definition: an MSP would be any financial institution with a substantial position in any major swap category, or any financial entity that was highly leveraged.[42] This approach (together with changes to the clearing exemption limiting the exemption to nonfinancial entities) appeared likely to capture many swaps between dealers and other financial institutions, which make up more than half of the swap market.

Eliminating the clearing exemption for financial entities and bringing more financial firms under the MSP definition, as the Senate-passed bill did, had the potential to bring nearly all of the swaps trading under the new regulatory regime—the 38% of trades between dealers and the 44% between dealers and other financial institutions.[43] This approach did raise questions of equity, that is, should a small community bank or credit union be subject to more stringent regulation than a giant nonfinancial corporation with a much greater volume of swaps outstanding?

The final version of the legislation made several changes to the MSP definition and the clearing requirement. The "highly leveraged" prong of the MSP definition was amended to clarify that it did not apply to regulated depository institutions, which are normally highly leveraged. In addition, as noted above, regulators were given discretion to exempt certain financial institutions with less than $10 billion in assets from the mandatory clearing requirement. The precise number of firms that named MSPs (and the proportion of swaps that would ultimately be cleared) would depend on the SEC and CFTC rulemakings required by the act.

On May 23, 2012, the CFTC and SEC released a joint final rule further defining the terms "swap dealer" and "major swap participant."[44] The final rule defines what constitutes a "substantial" position in swaps, for the purposes of being an MSP. The regulators propose a two-pronged test for a "substantial" position. "Current exposure," or the current mark-to-market value of a swaps or security-based swaps position, minus the value of collateral posted against the position, constitutes a "substantial position" if the net uncollateralized exposure exceeds $1 billion, or $3 billion for interest rate or currency swaps. The second test also involves a calculation, this time relating to future exposure. This is calculated by discounting current notional exposure by a risk factor, by the existence of netting agreements, and according to whether the position is cleared or subject to daily margining. A future exposure is "substantial" if it exceeds $2 billion, or $6 billion for interest or currency rate swaps. These quantitative tests for "substantial position" are meant to set a threshold "materially below" the level at which a swaps trader's default could pose a threat to the financial system.

In the joint final rule, the CFTC's and SEC's definition of a swap dealer closely follows the Dodd-Frank definition of a swap dealer.[45] The final rule defines a "swap dealer" as any person (a person, in this case, can be an entity) who holds himself out as a dealer in swaps; makes a market in swaps; regularly enters into swaps with counterparties as an ordinary course of business for his own account; or engages in activity causing himself to be commonly known as a dealer or market maker in swaps. The rule also excludes certain swaps used to hedge or mitigate risk, if the risks arise from a potential change in the value of assets a person owns or produces, or services the person provides. It also excludes swaps entered into between majority-owned affiliates. At the same time, the rule includes a de minimus exception. In order for a person to be regarded as a swap dealer, the aggregate gross notional amount of the swaps the person entered into during the prior 12 months in connection with swap dealing activities must exceed $8 billion during a phase-in period. The phase-in period would last two and a half years from the time data starts being reported to swap data repositories. After this time, the CFTC will undertake a study of the swap markets, and may reduce this de minimus amount to $3 billion, or may propose a new rule for a different de minimus threshold.

Reporting of Swaps and Security-Based Swaps

Swaps must be reported to registered swap data repositories or the CFTC.[46] Security-based swaps must be reported to registered security-based swap data repositories or to the SEC.[47] The Dodd-Frank Act requires all swaps to be reported.[48] Swaps and security-based swaps entered into prior to the date of the enactment of Dodd-Frank Act are exempt from the clearing requirement if they are reported in accordance with the act. Swaps and security-based swaps entered into after the enactment of the Dodd-Frank Act, but prior to the imposition of the clearing requirement, are exempt from the clearing requirement if they are reported in accordance with the act.

Section 727 of Dodd-Frank outlines the public availability of swap transaction data.[49] The CFTC is required to promulgate rules regarding the public availability of such data. Swaps that are subject to the clearing requirement, and swaps that are not subject to the clearing requirement, but are nonetheless cleared at registered derivatives clearing organizations, must have real-time reporting for such transactions. Real-time reporting means to report data relating to a swap transaction, including price and volume, as soon as technologically practicable after the time at which the swap transaction has been executed. For swaps that are not cleared and are reported pursuant to subsection (h)(6) (requiring reporting prior to the implementation of the clearing requirement), real-time reporting is required in a manner that does not disclose the business transactions and market positions of any person. Lastly, for swaps that are determined to be required to be cleared under subsection (h)(2) (outlining the two ways, discussed above, in which swaps may become subject to the clearing requirement), but are not cleared, real-time public reporting is required as well. There is no parallel requirement in the act for security-based swaps, presumably because national securities exchanges upon which these transactions will be executed already provide comparable reporting.[50]

The act also creates reporting obligations for uncleared swaps and security-based swaps (including swaps and security-based swaps that qualify for the end-user exemption).[51] Swaps entered into prior to the enactment of the act will be subject to reporting and recordkeeping requirements for uncleared swaps and security-based swaps.[52] The purpose of these requirements, presumably, is to give the relevant commissions access to a more complete picture of the derivatives market, even for swaps that are not required to be cleared.

The SEC proposed its rule on reporting requirements for security-based swaps, which was published on December 2, 2010.[53] Regulation SBSR (for "security-based swap reporting") would require security-based swap data repositories to register with the SEC as securities information processors, an existing category of regulated entity. The data that the repositories receive will fall into two categories: one to be made public and the other non-public. Information to be disclosed to the public will include

- information on the asset class and the underlying security;
- the price and notional amount of the security-based swap;
- the time of execution; and
- the effective and expiration dates of the security-based swap.
- Non-public information—to be available to the SEC—includes
- the identity of the swap counterparty, the broker, and the trading desk;
- any up-front payments;
- the title of the master agreement (if any);
- a description of the valuation methods to be used; and
- which counterparty will report the contract to the data repository.

Some market participants expressed concerns that "real-time" reporting (required by the statute, but left to the regulators to define) would be unduly burdensome for large or illiquid trades, where reporting might result in the disclosure of market-sensitive information about holders of large positions and their trading intentions. The SEC, however, proposed a narrow definition of "real-time"—"as soon as technologically practicable after the time at which the ... transaction has been executed."[54]

There are only a few circumstances where the real-time reporting requirement is qualified. In the case of contracts that are not required to be cleared and are not cleared, public reporting for such transactions shall not disclose the business transactions and market positions of any person. In addition, the SEC proposal does not address block trades directly, but notes that the SEC intends to propose a rule for reporting of block trades at a later date, after considering comments.[55]

On April 3, 2012, the CFTC issued a final rule describing reporting, recordkeeping and daily trading records obligations for swap dealers and

MSPs.[56] The CFTC's final rule followed a proposed rule released on December 23, 2010.[57] The CFTC's final rule calls for electronic reporting to a swap data repository (SDR) of swap data from each of two important stages of the existence of a swap: the creation of the swap, and the continuation of the swap over its existence until its final termination or expiration. The purpose of this appears to be to create an electronic audit trail of all stages of the swap.[58] The final rule requires swap dealers and MSPs to maintain records of all activities related to the business of the swap dealers or MSPs, regardless of whether they also have a prudential, or banking, regulator, with separate recordkeeping requirements.

Prevention of Evasion

The CFTC and SEC have the authority under the Dodd-Frank Act to promulgate rules the commissions determine to be necessary to "prevent evasions of the mandatory clearing requirements under this Act." However, this rulemaking authority, while broad, carries additional nuance described below.

As noted above, the statutory scheme of Dodd-Frank creates two ways in which a swap or security-based swap may become subject to the clearing requirement. In one scenario, derivatives clearing organizations and clearing agencies submit the swaps and security-based swaps they intend to clear to the CFTC or SEC and the agency determines whether to apply the clearing requirement to the transactions. In the other scenario, the CFTC and SEC are required to engage in an ongoing independent review of swaps and security-based swaps under their jurisdiction to determine whether those transactions should be subject to the mandatory clearing requirement. It is thus possible that the CFTC and SEC could identify swaps and security-based swaps that "would otherwise be subject to the clearing requirement" but for the fact that no derivatives clearing organization or clearing agency accepts them for clearing.

In that event, the relevant agency (CFTC for swaps, and SEC for security-based swaps) is required to investigate the relevant facts and circumstances, issue a public report of its investigation, and "take such actions as the Commission determines to be necessary and in the public interest, which may include requiring the retaining of adequate margin or capital by parties to the swap [or security-based swap], group, category, type, or class of swaps [or security-based swaps]."[59] However, neither the CFTC nor the SEC may "adopt rules requiring a derivatives clearing organization [or clearing agency] to list for clearing a swap, group, category, type, or class of swaps if the clearing of the swap, group, category, type, or class of swaps would threaten the financial integrity of the derivatives organization."[60]

Because the clearing requirement has not yet been fully implemented, it does not appear that the CFTC has exercised rulemaking authority pursuant to these provisions. However, in its rule proposal for implementing Dodd-Frank's clearing requirement, the CFTC also includes a proposal of rules for the prevention of evasion of the clearing requirement.[61] A final rule has not yet been issued.

The SEC, however, has issued its rules implementing Dodd-Frank's clearing requirement, and among those rules were certain provisions intended to prevent evasion of the clearing requirement.[62] For example, the SEC recognized that some entities may provide different clearing functions, but that those functions were not always the equivalent of "central clearing" of security-based swaps by a central counterparty (CCP). As a result, the SEC has issued a rule that requires market participants to submit security-based swaps to clearing agencies that function as CCPs.

ENHANCED CFTC AUTHORITY OVER COMMODITIES MARKETS

In 2008, as energy and grain prices set new records, speculators in derivatives were blamed by some for price volatility and for price levels that many observers believed were not justified by the underlying economic fundamentals. Although the CFTC maintained that markets were functioning normally and that the price discovery process was not being distorted, the 110th Congress considered legislation intended to insulate commodity prices from the impact of excessive speculation and manipulation. Congress implemented this goal by including a number of provisions in Title VII of the Dodd-Frank Act that enhanced the authority of the CFTC to police these markets and impose limits where the agency saw a need. To this end, Congress enhanced the CFTC's power to set margin and position limits and also amended the CFTC's authority to prohibit manipulation in markets for commodities and swaps. What follows is a brief description of the current status of these enhanced authorities.

Margin Requirements

Section 736 of the Dodd-Frank Act granted the CFTC the authority to set margin requirements for futures exchanges, as the CFTC finds to be necessary and appropriate for the protection of persons producing, handling, processing, or consuming any commodity traded for future delivery, or for the protection of traders or to insure fair dealing in commodities traded for future delivery.[63] The CFTC may set margin at certain registered entities under the condition that the rule or order issued by the agency be limited to protecting the financial integrity of a DCO, be designed for risk management purposes to protect financial integrity of transactions, and not set specific margin amounts. It does not appear that the CFTC has had occasion to use this authority since the passage of the act.

Position Limits

Section 737 of the Dodd-Frank Act appeared to direct the CFTC to establish position limits for swaps and futures. The law says that "the Commission shall by rule, regulation, or order establish limits on the amount of positions, as appropriate, other than bona fide hedge positions, that may be held by any person."[64] Believing this language required the CFTC to set position limits, regardless of whether position limits were determined to be necessary or appropriate to curb speculation in a given market, the CFTC approved rules setting position limits for certain commodities in November of 2011.[65] Industry groups challenged the regulations in court, arguing that Section 737 amended a broader statute, and, when analyzed in the proper statutory context, the CFTC was only required to set position limit rules where the Commission had found the rules to be necessary and appropriate for the market upon which the rules were imposed. The opponents of the position limit rules argued the rules issued by the CFTC violated the Commodity Exchange Act because the CFTC had not conducted the appropriate analysis to determine whether the rules were necessary and appropriate prior to issuing the rules.

The U.S. District Court for the District of Columbia vacated and remanded the CFTC's position limit rules in a decision issued in September of 2012.[66] Courts usually defer to the interpretation of the agency charged with implementing a statute, but only if the agency has reasonably interpreted an ambiguity that the agency acknowledges exists in the statute.[67] Here, the court could not give deference to the CFTC's interpretation of the statute, because the agency had erroneously found the statute to be unambiguous.[68] As a result of the court's decision to vacate the rules, the agency must now determine whether position limits are required by the act regardless of whether the limits are found by the agency to be necessary, prior to promulgating new rules.

Anti-Manipulation Authority

Section 753 also amended the Commodity Exchange Act (CEA) to broaden the CFTC's anti-manipulation authority and add new prohibitions against false reporting and providing misleading information to the CFTC.[69] Following the enactment of Dodd-Frank, Section 6(c)(1) of the CEA now provides that

> It shall be unlawful for any person directly or indirectly to use or employ or attempt to use or employ, in connection with any swap or a contract of sale of any commodity in interstate commerce, or for future delivery on or subject to the rules of any registered entity, any manipulative or deceptive device or contrivance, in contravention of such rules and regulations as the Commission shall promulgate ... [70]

The CFTC has issued regulations implementing this authority.[71] In its order adopting the new regulations, the CFTC likened the language in this section to Section 10b of the Securities Exchange Act of 1934 and to the Securities and Exchange Commission's rule 10b-5, implementing Section 10b. Section 10b, according to the Supreme Court, was designed as a "catchall clause to prevent fraudulent practices."[72] The CFTC determined that the language of CEA Section 6(c)(1) was designed to operate similarly as a catchall to prevent fraudulent practices in violation of the CEA.[73] The CFTC found, therefore, that, to the extent possible, the CFTC would interpret violations of Section 6(c)(1) similarly to violations of Section 10b and would base its analysis on the well-established body of law developed pursuant to Section 10b and Rule 10b-5. As a result, the CFTC decided to implement its new anti-manipulation authority flexibly, in keeping with the remedial purpose of the act. This case-by-case approach, rather than setting detailed rules, is also similar to the SEC's approach to prosecuting securities fraud.

The CFTC has had occasion to use this new authority to obtain settlements with market participants. In data released on October 5, 2012, the CFTC revealed that it had, among other enforcement actions, imposed the largest fine for violations of the anti-manipulation provisions of the CEA in CFTC history in 2012.[74] In that case, Barclays Bank, PLC had admitted to both United Kingdom and United States regulators that the bank had submitted false reports of its borrowing rates to the British Bankers Association (BBA) for the U.S. London Interbank Offered Rate ("LIBOR"), an index that purports to measure the interest rates at which banks may borrow funds from each other. Barclays admitted, at times, to submitting knowingly false rates at the request of some of the bank's derivative traders, when the traders believed that a higher or lower LIBOR would improve their position on certain investments. Barclays also admitted that during the financial crisis it began to suspect that other member banks that were submitting rates to the BBA were understating their borrowing costs. In order to manage public perception of the bank and to prevent investors from questioning the health of the bank, Barclay's began to report borrowing costs to the BBA that were below the bank's actual borrowing costs. The CFTC found, based upon its investigation into the matter, that Barclays was likely guilty of violating Section 6(c)(1) of the CEA.[75] In its agreement with the CFTC, Barclays did not admit to violating the CEA, but has agreed to pay a $200 million fine and to comply with certain internal controls designed to prevent future LIBOR manipulation stipulated by the CFTC in its order. With the broader authority to prevent and prosecute fraudulent activity provided to the CFTC in the Dodd-Frank Act, enforcement actions similar to the Barclay's fine are expected in the future.[76]

SECTION 716—PROHIBITION ON FEDERAL ASSISTANCE TO SWAPS ENTITIES

Section 716 originated in the Senate Agriculture Committee and was included in the bill that passed the Senate in May 2010. The section prohibited federal assistance, defined as the use of any funds to loan money to, buy the securities or other assets of, or to enter into "any assistance arrangement" with a "swaps entity." Swaps entities included swap dealers and major swap participants (and the equivalents in security-based swaps), securities and futures exchanges, SEFs, and clearing organizations registered with the CFTC, the SEC, or any other federal or state agency.

The intent of the provision was to ensure that taxpayer funds would not have to be used to meet obligations of financial institutions engaged in risky derivatives trading. Such activity was deemed too risky to be under the federal safety net that covers insured depository institutions. The Chairwoman of the Senate Agriculture Committee at the time, Senator Lincoln explained it this way:

> This provision seeks to ensure that banks get back to the business of banking. Under our current system, there are a handful of big banks that are simply no longer acting like banks.... In my view, banks were never intended to perform these [derivatives] activities, which have been the single largest factor to these institutions growing so large that taxpayers had no choice but to bail them out in order to prevent total economic ruin.[77]

Supporters of the original version of Section 716 described it as an appropriate means to compel banks to spin off their swap dealings, or to "push them out" into separately capitalized affiliates. Opponents of the measure argued that the definitions of federal assistance and swaps entity were so broadly drafted that there might be unanticipated consequences. For example, if Citigroup sold off its swap dealer operations, it would still have hundreds of billions of loans and other risky assets on its balance sheet, which it would need to hedge with interest rate swaps and other derivatives. This hedging activity would likely put the bank into the major swap participant category, and thus foreclose access to the discount window, FDIC insurance, and other features of the safety net. Similarly, if the Federal Reserve were supplying liquidity to the financial system during a future crisis, would it be prudent to deny such support to clearinghouses which represent concentrations of risk?

The conference committee adopted a modified version of Section 716, which narrowed the definitions of swaps entity and permitted banks to act as swap dealers under some circumstances. In the final legislation, exchanges, SEFs, and clearing organizations are not swaps entities. In addition, the term "swaps entity" does not include a major swap participant or major security-based swap participant that is an insured depository institution.

The final version clarifies that the prohibition on aid does not prevent a bank from creating an affiliate that is a swaps entity, provided that the affiliate complies with sections 23A and 23B of the Federal Reserve Act and other requirements of the Fed, the SEC, and the CFTC. Moreover, the bank itself may continue to act as a swaps dealer for contracts involving rates or reference assets that are permissible for investment by a national bank. This means that banks can continue as dealers in swaps linked to interest rates, currencies, government securities, and precious metals, but not other commodities or equities. Credit default swaps are treated as a special category: banks may deal in them if they are cleared by a derivatives clearing organization regulated by the SEC or CFTC. Dealing in uncleared credit default swaps, however, is not deemed to be a permissible bank activity.

Finally, Section 716 mandates that no taxpayer funds may be used to prevent the liquidation of a swaps entity. Any funds expended in such a liquidation proceeding, and not covered by the swaps entity's assets, may be recouped through assessments on the financial sector.

Section 716 has not taken effect yet. A guidance issued by the Office of the Comptroller of the Currency, the Board of Governors of the Federal Reserve, and the Federal Deposit Insurance Corporation has indicated that Section 716 will not take effect until July 16, 2013.[78]

End Notes

[1] For a description of the mechanics of these contracts, see CRS Report R40646, Derivatives Regulation and Legislation Through the 111th Congress, by Rena S. Miller.

2 See Bank for International Settlements (BIS), Table 23B, for year 2000 turnover for derivative financial instruments traded on organized exchanges, available at http://www.bis.org/publ/qtrpdf/r_qa0206.pdf. For December 2008 figures for derivatives traded on organized exchanges, see BIS Quarterly Review, September 2009, International Banking and Financial Market Developments, available at http://www.bis.org/publ/qtrpdf/r_qt0909.pdf.

[3] See Bank for International Settlements (BIS), Statistical Annex, Table 19, December, 2000 figure for notional amount of total OTC contracts, available at http://www.bis.org/ publ/qtrpdf/r_qa0206.pdf. See Bank for International Settlements (BIS), BIS Quarterly Review, September 2009, Statistical Annex, Table 19, for December 2008 figure for notional amount of total OTC contracts, available at http://www.bis.org/publ/qtrpdf/r_qa0909.pdf.

[4] Federal Reserve, Flow of Funds Accounts of the United States, September 17, 2009, accessible at http://www.federalreserve.gov/releases/z1/Current/z1r-1.pdf.

[5] See Bank for International Settlements, "Statistical Release: OTC Derivatives Statistics at end-December 2011," published May, 2012. For additional details on OTC derivatives market trends over time, please see their chart on page 2. Available at http://www.bis.org/publ/otc_hy1205.pdf.

[6] Ibid.

[7] Also referred to as a central counterparty or as a derivatives clearing organization (DCO).

[8] See CRS Report R41350, The Dodd-Frank Wall Street Reform and Consumer Protection Act: Issues and Summary, coordinated by Baird Webel.

[9] The credit events that trigger credit swap payments may include ratings downgrades, debt restructuring, late payment of interest or principal, as well as default.

[10] For an account of this process, see Office of the Special Inspector General for the Troubled Asset Relief Program ("SIGTARP"), Factors Affecting Efforts to Limit Payments to AIG Counterparties, November 17, 2009.

[11] 17 Fed. Reg. 48208, available at http://www.cftc.gov/ucm/groups/public/ @lrfederalregister/ documents/file/2012- 18003a.pdf.

[12] Section 723 of the Dodd-Frank Act (codified at 7 U.S.C. §2).

[13] Section 763(a) of the Dodd-Frank Act (codified at 15 U.S.C. § 78a et seq.).

[14] Section 723(a)(3) of the Dodd-Frank Act (codified at 7 U.S.C. §2(h)(1)) (swaps); Section 763(a) of the Dodd-Frank Act (codified at 15 U.S.C. § 78a et seq.)(security-based swaps).

[15] Section 723(a)(3) of the Dodd-Frank Act (codified at 7 U.S.C. §2(h)(2)) (swaps); Section 763(a) of the Dodd-Frank Act (codified at 15 U.S.C. § 78a et seq.)(security-based swaps).

[16] 17 Fed. Reg. 48208, available at http://www.cftc.gov/ucm/groups/public/@lrfederalregister/ documents/file/2012- 18003a.pdf.

[17] Rules for the registration and regulation of derivatives clearing organizations are enacted by Section 725 of the Dodd-Frank Act (codified at 7 U.S.C. §7a-1). The CFTC has implemented this section further defining entities that are considered DCOs. 76 Fed. Reg. 69334, available at http://www.cftc.gov/ucm/groups/public/@lrfederalregister/ documents/ file/2011-27536a.pdf.

[18] Rules for the registration and regulation of clearing agencies were enacted by Section 763(b) of the Dodd-Frank Act (codified at 15 U.S.C. §78a-1). The SEC rulemaking process regarding clearing agency standards is ongoing. The agency has proposed rules to implement registration requirements and other standards, available at http://www.sec.gov/ rules/proposed/2011/34-64017.pdf.

[19] Section 723(a)(3) of the Dodd-Frank Act (codified at 7 U.S.C. §2(h)) (swaps); Section 763(a) of the Dodd-Frank Act (codified at 15 U.S.C. § 78a et seq.)(security-based swaps). Similar considerations were mandated by the Senate passed version of the bill, but those considerations were to be applied to the agencies' rulemakings to identify other classes of transactions that should be subject to the clearing requirement that had not been submitted to the agency. Section 723(a) of H.R. 4173 (as passed by the Senate).

[20] Section 723(a)(3) of the Dodd-Frank Act (codified at 7 U.S.C. §2(h)(3)) (swaps); Section 763(a) of the Dodd-Frank Act (codified at 15 U.S.C. § 78a et seq.)(security-based swaps).

[21] Section 723(a)(3) of the Dodd-Frank Act (codified at 7 U.S.C. §2(h)(8)); Section 763(a) of the Dodd-Frank Act (codified at 15 U.S.C. § 78a et seq.)(security-based swaps).

[22] 77 Fed. Reg. 47170 (August 7, 2012) available at http://www.cftc.gov/ucm/groups/public/ @lrfederalregister/ documents/file/2012-18382a.pdf.

[23] SEC, Process for Submissions for Review of Security-Based Swaps for Mandatory Clearing and Notice Filing Requirements for Clearing Agencies; Technical Amendments to Rule 19b-4 and Form 19b-4 Applicable to All Self Regulatory Organizations, Final Rule, Release No. 34-67286 (June 28, 2012) available at http://www.sec.gov/rules/ final/2012/34-67286.pdf.

[24] Section 723 of the Dodd-Frank Act (new section 5h(e) of the Commodity Exchange Act to be codified after 7 U.S.C. §7b-2).

[25] Only eligible contract participants will be able to trade on SEFs and SBSEFs.

[26] Section 720 of S. 3217, as reported by the Senate Committee on Banking, Housing, and Urban Affairs, April 15, 2010.

[27] Section 720 of the Dodd-Frank Act, P.L. 111-203.

[28] Commodity Futures Trading Commission, "Core Principles and Other Requirements for Swap Execution Facilities," Vol. 76 No. 5, Federal Register p. 1214, January 7, 2011. And at 17 C.F.R. § 37.

[29] See Commodity Futures Trading Commission, "Core Principles and Other Requirements for Swap Execution Facilities," Vol. 76 No. 5, Federal Register p. 1214, January 7, 2011, at p. 1219.

[30] SEC, "Registration and Regulation of Security-Based Swap Execution Facilities," (Release No. 34-63825; File No. S7-06-11), February 2, 2011 available at http://sec.gov/rules/proposed/2011/34-63825.pdf.

[31] Section 723(a)(3) of the Dodd-Frank Act (codified at 7 U.S.C. §2(h)(7)) (swaps); Section 763(a) of the Dodd-Frank Act (codified at 15 U.S.C. § 78a et seq.)(security-based swaps).

[32] Id.

[33] Section 723(a)(3) of the Dodd-Frank Act (codified at 7 U.S.C. §2(h)(7)) (swaps); Section 763(a) of the Dodd-Frank Act (codified at 15 U.S.C. § 78a et seq.)(security-based swaps). (page 822 and 1060).

[34] Ben Protess, In New Rules to Shine Light on Derivatives, Regulators Also Allow Exemptions, DealBook NYTimes Blog (July 10, 2012), http://dealbook.nytimes.com/2012/07/10/in-new-rules-to-shine-light-on-derivatives-regulatorsalso-allow-exemptions/.

[35] Affiliates of persons qualifying for the end user exception are not eligible to engage in swaps or security-based swaps on the behalf of qualifying persons if the affiliate is a swap dealer, security-based swap dealer, major swap participant, major security-based swap participant, companies that would be investment companies under section 3 of the Investment Company Act of 1940 but for the exceptions provided in subparagraphs (c)(1) or (c)(7) of that section (15 U.S.C. §80a-3), a commodity pool, or a bank holding company with over $50, 000,000,000 in consolidated assets. Section 723(a)(3) of the Dodd-Frank Act (codified at 7 U.S.C. §2(h)(3)) (swaps); Section 763(a) of the Dodd-Frank Act (codified at 15 U.S.C. § 78a et seq.)(security-based swaps).

[36] Section 723(a)(3) of the Dodd-Frank Act (codified at 7 U.S.C. §2(h)(7)) (swaps); Section 763(a) of the Dodd-Frank Act (codified at 15 U.S.C. § 78a et seq.)(security-based swaps). The CFTC has also issued rules implementing Section 723, available at http://www.cftc.gov/ucm/groups/public/@newsroom/documents/file/federalregister071012.pdf.

[37] CFTC, End User Exception to the Clearing Requirement for Swaps, RIN 3038-AD10 (September 17, 2012) available at http://www.cftc.gov/ucm/groups /public/ @ newsroom/documents/file/federalregister071012.pdf.

[38] Section 723(a)(3) of the Dodd-Frank Act (codified at 7 U.S.C. §2(h)(7)) (swaps); Section 763(a) of the Dodd-Frank Act (codified at 15 U.S.C. § 78a et seq.)(security-based swaps).

[39] SEC, End-User Exception to the Clearing Requirement for Security-Based Swaps, Docket No. 34-63556 (December 15, 2010) available at http://www.sec.gov/rules/proposed/2010/34-63556.pdf.

[40] Section 3101 of H.R. 4173, as passed the House of Representatives, December 11, 2009.

[41] Section 711 of S. 3217, as reported by the Senate Committee on Banking, Housing, and Urban Affairs, April 15, 2010.

[42] This was not a "net" position, and applied to individual categories of swaps, as opposed to the institution's aggregate swaps book.

[43] The 38% and 44% figures are based on BIS data released in May 2010 for total global notional amounts outstanding as of December, 2009. Since much of the drafting of the bills that ultimately became the Dodd-Frank Act occurred prior to May, 2010, prior figures using earlier data may have looked slightly different. The May 2010 BIS data is available at http://www.bis.org/statistics/otcder/dt1920a.pdf.

[44] Commodity Futures Trading Commission and the Securities and Exchange Commission, "Further Definition of 'Swap Dealer,'" "Major Swap Participant," and "Eligible Contract

Participant." 77 Federal Register 30596, May 23, 2012. Available at http://www.cftc.gov/ucm/groups/public/@lrfederalregister/documents/file/2012-10562a.pdf.

[45] Section 721 of the Dodd-Frank Act.

[46] Section 723(a)(3) of the Dodd-Frank Act (to be codified at 7 U.S.C. §2(h)(5)).

[47] Section 763(a) of the Dodd-Frank Act (to be codified at 15 U.S.C. § 78a et seq.).

[48] Sections 3103 and 3203 of H.R. 4173 (as passed); Sections 723(a) and 763 of S. 3217 (as passed).

[49] Section 725 of the Dodd-Frank Act (to be codified at 7 U.S.C. §2(a)).

[50] See 15 U.S.C. § 78f.

[51] Section 729 of the Dodd-Frank Act (to be codified at 7 U.S.C. §6o-1) and Section 766 of the Dodd-Frank Act (to be codified at 15 U.S.C. §78a et seq.).

[52] Id.

[53] SEC, "Regulation SBSR – Reporting and Dissemination of Security-Based Swap Information," (Release No. 34- 63346; File No. S7-34-10), Federal Register, v. 75, December 2, 2010, p. 75208.

[54] Ibid., p. 75210.

[55] Block trades are very large securities transactions, which would be expected to move prices if they were executed on a public exchange. Securities markets have developed a number of mechanisms to match large buyers and sellers without revealing the size of the deal to the public markets, which would raise the cost of the transaction to the block traders. These include the upstairs market and dark pools, where block trades can be negotiated out of the public eye.

[56] Commodity Futures Trading Commission, "Swap Dealer and Major Swap Participant Recordkeeping, Reporting and Duties Rules," 77 Federal Register 20128, April 3, 2012. Available at http://www.cftc.gov/ucm/groups/public/@lrfederalregister/documents/ file/2012-5317a.pdf.

[57] CFTC, "17 CFR Part 49: Swap Data Repositories," Federal Register, v. 75, December 23, 2010, p. 80897.

[58] See Commodity Futures Trading Commission, "Swap Dealer and Major Swap Participant Recordkeeping, Reporting and Duties Rules," 77 Federal Register 20128, April 3, 2012 at p. 20212: "Appendix 2: Statement of Chairman Gary Gensler."

[59] Section 723(a)(3) of the Dodd-Frank Act (codified at 7 U.S.C. §2(h)(4)) (swaps); Section 763(a) of the Dodd-Frank Act (codified at 15 U.S.C. § 78a et seq.)(security-based swaps).

[60] Section 723(a)(3) of the Dodd-Frank Act (codified at 7 U.S.C. §2(h)(4)) (swaps); Section 763(a) of the Dodd-Frank Act (codified at 15 U.S.C. § 78a et seq.)(security-based swaps).

[61] 77 Fed. Reg. 47170 (August 7, 2012) available at http://www.cftc.gov/ucm/groups/public/@lrfederalregister/ documents/file/2012-18382a.pdf.

[62] SEC, Process for Submissions for Review of Security-Based Swaps for Mandatory Clearing and Notice Filing Requirements for Clearing Agencies; Technical Amendments to Rule 19b-4 and Form 19b-4 Applicable to All Self Regulatory Organizations, Final Rule, Release No. 34-67286 (June 28, 2012) available at http://www.sec.gov/rules/ final/2012/34-67286.pdf.

[63] Codified at 7 U.S.C. §12a(7).

[64] Codified at 7 U.S.C. §6a(a).

[65] 76 Fed. Reg. 7126 (November 18, 2011) available at http://www.cftc.gov/ucm/groups/public/@lrfederalregister/documents/file/2011-28809a.pdf.

[66] International Swaps and Derivatives Association v. CFTC, Civil Action No. 11-cv-2146 (RLW), 2012 U.S. Dist. LEXIS 139788 (U.S.D.C. September 28, 2012).

[67] Peter Pan Bus Lines v. Feds Motor Carrier Safety Administration, 471 F.2d 1350 (D.C. Cir. 2006).

[68] International Swaps and Derivatives Association v. CFTC, Civil Action No. 11-cv-2146 (RLW), 2012 U.S. Dist. LEXIS 139788 (U.S.D.C. September 28, 2012).

[69] Section 729 of the Dodd-Frank Act (codified at 7 U.S.C. §9).

[70] codified at 7 U.S.C. §9.

[71] 76 Fed. Reg. 41398 (July 14, 2011).

[72] Chiarella v. U.S. 445 U.S. 222, 226 (1980).

[73] 76 Fed. Reg. 41398 (July 14, 2011).

[74] CFTC, CFTC Releases Enforcement Division's Annual Results, October 5, 2012, available at http://www.cftc.gov/ PressRoom/PressReleases/pr6378-12.

[75] In the Matter of Barclay's, PLCOrder Instituting Proceedings Pursuant to Section 6(c) and 6(d) of the Commodity Exchange Act, As Amended, Making Findings, and Imposing Remedial Sanctions, CFTC Docket No. 12-25 (June 27, 2012) available at http://www.cftc.gov/ ucm/ groups/public/@lrenforcementactions/documents/legalpleading/ enfbarclaysorder062712.pdf.

[76] Peter J. Henning, CFTC is Set to Get Tougher on Fraud, NYTimes Blog, (November 1, 2010) available at http://dealbook.nytimes.com/2010/11/01/c-f-t-c-is-set-to-get-tougher-on-fraud/.

[77] Remarks of Senator Blanche Lincoln, Congressional Record, May 5, 2010, p. S3140.

[78] 77 Fed. Reg. 27456 (May 10, 2012), available at http://www.gpo.gov/fdsys/pkg/FR-2012-05-10/pdf/2012-11326.pdf.

INDEX

A

access, 2, 7, 39, 52, 53, 54, 62, 65, 78, 79, 83, 85, 96, 97, 104, 110
accommodations, 24
AD, 38, 43
adjustment, 86
agencies, 3, 5, 7, 9, 12, 17, 18, 20, 21, 23, 26, 27, 28, 33, 34, 48, 84, 88, 94, 105, 106, 112
agriculture, 89
American Stock Exchange, 12
assessment, 56, 72
assets, vii, 1, 8, 13, 78, 79, 90, 98, 102, 109, 110, 111, 113
audit, 15, 55, 96, 105
authenticity, 15
authority(s), 2, 3, 4, 9, 16, 17, 19, 20, 22, 23, 24, 25, 26, 27, 28, 29, 43, 46, 51, 60, 61, 64, 67, 69, 71, 73, 75, 76, 85, 94, 105, 106, 107, 108
average revenue, 72

B

background information, 39
bail, 110
balance sheet, 110
Bank Secrecy Act, 15
banking, 4, 9, 14, 16, 18, 20, 22, 23, 24, 30, 36, 42, 43, 47, 50, 84, 98, 105, 110
bankruptcy, 3, 58, 93
banks, 7, 11, 18, 30, 31, 32, 36, 41, 60, 79, 85, 98, 101, 109, 110
base, 57, 108
Belgium, 8, 36, 42
benefits, 39, 54, 59, 60, 74
bonds, viii, 2, 6, 11, 12, 31, 90
breakdown, 5
business model, 96
businesses, 89
buyer(s), 3, 11, 14, 77, 114

C

cash, 8, 9, 33, 35, 39, 88, 89, 96
central bank, 7, 16, 18, 19, 23, 33, 60, 73, 78
certification, 71
CFR, 47, 72, 74, 75, 114
chaos, 93
Chicago, 6, 32
Chicago Mercantile Exchange, 6
circulation, 9
clarity, 64
classes, 112
Code of Federal Regulations, 47, 71
collateral, 23, 34, 41, 46, 56, 60, 62, 66, 68, 69, 80, 91, 92, 102

commerce, 108
commercial, viii, 2, 9, 12, 32, 34, 36, 88, 97, 98, 100, 101
commodity, 20, 21, 47, 89, 98, 106, 107, 108, 113
commodity futures, 20, 47
community, 101
competition, 53, 69, 74, 95, 96
competitive advantage, 69, 74
competitors, 69, 74
complexity, 59
compliance, 15, 17, 24, 25, 29, 55, 65, 72, 93, 96
computer, 14
conference, 110
conflict, 26, 55
conflict of interest, 55
Congress, 1, 2, 12, 13, 14, 16, 21, 22, 24, 25, 41, 43, 63, 87, 106, 111
consolidation, 14
construction, 90
consulting, 25
contingency, 78
controversial, 99
coordination, 2, 3, 19, 26, 27
correlation, 13
cost, 53, 61, 73, 79, 100, 114
counsel, 59
covering, 70
credit market, 89
credit rating, 93
creditors, viii, 87
creditworthiness, 89, 91
crises, 13
crisis management, 54
criticism, 63
CSD, 53, 56, 59
currency, viii, 2, 10, 33, 102
customers, 11, 13, 32, 33, 36, 39, 52, 60, 89, 95, 96

D

day-to-day transactions, vii, 2
Department of the Treasury, 9, 40, 43
deposit accounts, 24
depository institutions, 6, 7, 11, 17, 18, 24, 33, 34, 39, 98, 102, 110
deposits, 88
derivatives, viii, 2, 3, 4, 6, 8, 10, 11, 14, 16, 17, 18, 19, 20, 27, 28, 44, 46, 76, 87, 88, 89, 90, 93, 94, 95, 96, 98, 99, 100, 103, 104, 105, 106, 110, 111, 112, 113
derivatives market, viii, 3, 8, 20, 87, 88, 89, 90, 99, 104, 111
direct cost(s), 53
directors, 55
disaster, 62, 83
disbursement, 34
disclosure, 104
distribution, 89
District of Columbia, 107
Dodd-Frank Wall Street Reform and Consumer Protection Act, v, viii, 19, 38, 39, 40, 43, 45, 76, 87, 111
draft, 43

E

earnings, 24
economic fundamentals, 106
electronic systems, 96
emergency, 24, 68, 69, 72, 83, 96
emergency rule, 96
employees, 84
employment, 56
end-users, 36, 88, 101
energy, 89, 106
energy prices, 89
enforcement, 2, 24, 25, 26, 43, 109
engineering, 90
English Language, 86
equity(s), 6, 11, 12, 30, 100, 101, 111
examinations, 24, 25, 70
exclusion, 21, 67, 85
execution, 21, 24, 88, 95, 96, 97, 104
exercise, 25, 26, 27, 61
expenditures, 70
expertise, 94
exposure, 22, 56, 57, 58, 81, 88, 89, 102

F

fairness, 71
Fannie Mae, 101
FDIC, 110
federal agency, 7, 20, 29, 47
federal assistance, 109, 110
federal funds, 9, 33
federal government, 9, 12, 34, 40
Federal Register, 112, 113, 114
Federal Reserve, v, 2, 3, 4, 5, 6, 7, 8, 9, 11, 12, 13, 14, 16, 17, 19, 20, 21, 22, 24, 26, 27, 29, 30, 32, 33, 34, 35, 38, 39, 40, 41, 42, 43, 45, 48, 60, 69, 71, 73, 74, 75, 84, 86, 93, 110
Federal Reserve Board, 17, 20, 21, 22, 24, 75
financial condition, 89
financial crisis, vii, viii, 1, 2, 14, 19, 87, 88, 90, 109
financial firms, 101
financial innovation, 88
financial institutions, vii, 1, 2, 3, 4, 8, 9, 10, 11, 12, 13, 14, 15, 16, 19, 20, 21, 22, 23, 25, 27, 28, 29, 30, 31, 36, 39, 43, 46, 54, 57, 65, 88, 89, 92, 99, 101, 102, 109
financial intermediaries, 3, 14, 36
financial market utilities, viii, 45
financial markets, 12, 13, 23, 25, 49
financial resources, 56, 57, 62, 64, 65, 79, 81
financial sector, 14, 111
Financial Services Authority, 18, 38
financial stability, viii, 23, 25, 43, 46, 53, 60, 87
financial system, vii, 1, 2, 3, 12, 13, 16, 18, 20, 22, 25, 27, 43, 46, 52, 54, 60, 70, 72, 73, 88, 99, 100, 102, 110
flexibility, 71, 72
force, 69
foreign banks, 36
foreign exchange, 3, 6, 9, 19, 33, 89, 100
formation, 4
France, 42
fraud, 108, 115
Freddie Mac, 101
freezing, 89
funding, 19, 40
funds, vii, 2, 4, 6, 7, 8, 9, 10, 11, 14, 15, 33, 34, 35, 38, 50, 62, 66, 69, 75, 77, 79, 80, 95, 101, 109, 111

G

Germany, 42
globalization, 14
goods and services, 9
governance, 52, 54, 61, 62, 65, 78, 80, 85
government securities, 6, 7, 11, 12, 111
governments, 12, 40
grants, 2, 93
growth, 90
guidance, 13, 19, 44, 63, 64, 85, 100, 111
guidelines, 18
guilty, 109

H

hazards, 54
health, 109
hedging, 89, 90, 98, 99, 101, 110
history, 109
holding company, 113
House, 4, 6, 9, 20, 31, 36, 39, 41, 43, 100, 101, 113
House of Representatives, 4, 20, 113
housing, 90
housing boom, 90

I

ICE, 6, 16, 32
identity, 71, 104
image(s), 31, 69, 88
improvements, 74
independence, 55, 85
individuals, 15
industry, 3, 16, 17, 32, 47, 60, 62, 73, 75
information sharing, 17

infrastructure, vii, 1, 2, 3, 4, 5, 6, 8, 13, 16, 18, 28, 94
institutions, vii, 2, 3, 4, 7, 9, 10, 11, 12, 13, 15, 18, 19, 21, 24, 25, 26, 31, 33, 35, 36, 39, 46, 84, 92, 98, 102, 110
integrity, 74, 91, 106, 107
interest rates, 7, 89, 109, 110
interface, 10
intermediaries, 10, 21, 96
internal controls, 109
internal processes, 15
International Monetary Fund, 13, 40, 43
international standards, 17, 19, 23, 46, 48, 49, 68, 73, 84
intervention, viii, 88
investment(s), 21, 109, 110, 113
investors, 12, 32, 40, 109
issues, 19, 31, 52, 69, 72, 82, 85
Italy, 42

J

Japan, 42
jurisdiction, 16, 20, 32, 47, 72, 84, 94, 100, 105
justification, 72

L

large derivatives dealers, viii, 88
laws, 15, 20, 39, 47, 61, 73
lead, 5, 13, 15, 56
legislation, 20, 96, 101, 106, 110
lender of last resort, 4, 16
lending, 38
light, 5, 58, 71, 113
limited liability, 36
liquidity, viii, 2, 13, 15, 19, 20, 27, 46, 49, 50, 53, 65, 72, 78, 79, 80, 89, 94, 110
loans, 9, 34, 110

M

majority, 6, 11, 24, 75, 102
management, viii, 7, 15, 23, 27, 45, 46, 47, 48, 49, 50, 51, 52, 53, 54, 55, 56, 57, 59, 60, 65, 70, 71, 72, 73, 74, 76, 77, 78, 80, 81, 82, 83, 84, 85
manipulation, 96, 106, 108, 109
manufactured goods, 98
mark up, 20
market disruptions, vii, 1
market position, 74, 103, 104
market structure, 52, 93
marketplace, 31, 64, 90, 92
matter, 52, 67, 68, 73, 85, 109
measurement, 57, 58
membership, 18, 43, 57
merchandise, 98
messages, 15, 36
metals, 111
mission, 53
models, 55, 81, 85, 90
modifications, 85
monetary policy, 4, 7, 16
money supply, 7
mortgage-backed securities, 10, 30, 31, 93
Multilateral, 35

N

Netherlands, 36, 42
New York Stock Exchange, 12

O

Obama, 13, 16, 20
Obama Administration, 13, 16, 20
Office of Management and Budget, 75
open market operations, 7, 34
operating system, 52
operations, viii, 2, 7, 8, 23, 24, 27, 28, 45, 46, 47, 51, 55, 59, 60, 61, 62, 63, 64, 67, 69, 70, 72, 73, 74, 76, 77, 78, 79, 81, 83, 84, 88, 110
opportunities, 53
OTC market, viii, 87, 88, 89, 91, 92, 93, 95, 96

overlap, 8, 66
oversight, 3, 4, 5, 15, 16, 17, 19, 20, 21, 23, 26, 29, 60, 70, 74
over-the-counter (OTC), viii, 2, 20, 87, 88, 90
ownership, 10, 32, 57
ownership structure, 57

P

parallel, 51, 93, 97, 103
payment, clearing, and settlement (PCS), viii, 2, 4
payroll, vii, 2, 9, 31, 35, 36
permit, 50, 53, 54, 68, 78, 79, 95
platform, 84, 91, 95, 97
police, 106
policy, 7, 17, 19, 41, 42, 43, 48, 58, 61, 70, 71, 73, 85, 86
pools, 90, 114
portfolio, 32
President, 42
prevention, 106
principles, 17, 18, 46, 49, 60, 68, 71, 96
private sector, viii, 2, 3, 5, 7, 8, 9, 11, 16, 41, 70
product eligibility, 62
protection, 3, 107
prudential regulation, 99, 100
public interest, 17, 80, 105
public markets, 114
publishing, viii, 45

Q

questioning, 109

R

real estate, 9, 34
real time, 7, 11, 31
recommendations, 4, 19, 56
recovery, 62, 79, 83
recovery plan, 62, 83
reform(s), v, viii, 4, 13, 19, 20, 38, 39, 40, 42, 43, 45, 57, 76, 87, 88, 91, 93, 111
regional integration, 14
regulations, 23, 28, 46, 51, 59, 72, 84, 93, 99, 100, 107, 108
regulatory agencies, 16, 17
regulatory framework, 2, 4, 19, 20, 28
regulatory oversight, 4, 5, 20, 21
relevance, 50
reliability, 78
repo, viii, 2, 19, 31, 34, 41
reputation, 15
requirements, 2, 15, 19, 20, 23, 24, 26, 28, 29, 43, 46, 47, 51, 53, 54, 55, 56, 58, 60, 67, 68, 69, 70, 72, 74, 76, 79, 80, 81, 84, 85, 88, 93, 97, 99, 103, 104, 105, 107, 110, 112
resilience, 18
resources, 53, 56, 65, 83, 94, 96
response, 56
restructuring, 111
retail, 3, 4, 9, 19, 39, 49, 50, 51, 68, 85, 86
revenue, 14
rights, 62, 66
risk management, 15, 17, 18, 20, 21, 23, 25, 27, 28, 29, 46, 48, 52, 54, 60, 61, 62, 63, 65, 66, 85, 107
risk profile, 62, 63, 66
rules, viii, 17, 23, 24, 27, 28, 29, 31, 43, 44, 45, 47, 50, 51, 53, 54, 59, 61, 62, 64, 67, 68, 69, 70, 71, 72, 74, 76, 77, 78, 81, 83, 84, 94, 95, 96, 97, 99, 103, 105, 106, 107, 108, 112, 113, 114

S

safety, 12, 46, 52, 60, 70, 110
sanctions, 15
savings, 36
scope, 2, 21, 23, 25, 28, 29, 49, 52, 53, 62, 64, 65, 66, 69, 76, 84
Secretary of the Treasury, 21, 22, 24
securities, vii, 1, 3, 4, 6, 7, 8, 9, 10, 11, 12, 13, 18, 19, 20, 21, 30, 31, 32, 33, 34, 36, 38, 39, 40, 41, 43, 46, 47, 60, 62, 66, 72,

73, 76, 77, 78, 79, 80, 90, 93, 96, 103, 104, 108, 109, 111, 114
Securities Exchange Act, 46, 76, 108
securities firms, 32
security, 10, 15, 32, 40, 56, 78, 88, 90, 93, 94, 95, 97, 98, 99, 102, 103, 104, 105, 106, 109, 110, 112, 113, 114
seller(s), 11, 14, 77, 114
Senate, 20, 43, 96, 101, 109, 110, 112, 113
September 11, 18
service provider, 43, 69, 74
services, 3, 4, 6, 7, 8, 9, 11, 12, 16, 17, 24, 30, 31, 32, 33, 35, 36, 39, 43, 52, 53, 60, 62, 65, 66, 67, 69, 70, 72, 74, 80, 83, 84, 86, 96, 102
settlements, 10, 30, 49, 65, 78, 79, 108
shock, 89
Social Security, 35
speculation, 99, 106, 107
speculative positions, viii, 87
spillover effects, 13
spin, 110
stability, 13, 16, 20, 27, 43, 46, 52, 54, 60
state(s), 16, 17, 24, 26, 34, 46, 51, 52, 53, 54, 59, 60, 61, 64, 80, 85, 109
statistics, 38, 113
statutes, 59
statutory authority, 16, 64
statutory provisions, 28
stock, 89, 90
stock price, 89
storage, 34
stress, viii, 14, 16, 55, 57, 87
stress test, 57
structure, 53, 54, 55
substitutes, 8
supervision, vii, 2, 4, 12, 13, 16, 17, 18, 25, 27, 29, 46, 58, 63, 70
supervisor(s), 16, 26, 53, 55
suppliers, 8
Supreme Court, 108
Sweden, 42
Switzerland, 38, 39, 41, 42, 43, 44
systemic risk, viii, 2, 3, 5, 12, 13, 14, 15, 25, 40, 46, 52, 54, 55, 60, 69, 87, 95

T

taxes, 71
taxpayers, 60, 110
TDD, 86
technical assistance, 25
techniques, 55, 82
technology(s), 14, 29, 53, 62, 84
telecommunications, 7, 14
telephone, 36, 96, 97
time frame, 67
time periods, 22, 82
Title I, 92
Title II, 92
trade, 8, 9, 12, 13, 24, 31, 32, 39, 91, 92, 95, 96, 97, 112
trading partners, viii, 40, 87, 88
transaction costs, 60
transaction value, 9
transactions, vii, 1, 2, 3, 4, 5, 6, 7, 8, 9, 10, 11, 12, 14, 19, 20, 22, 23, 29, 30, 31, 32, 34, 35, 36, 39, 46, 50, 52, 54, 59, 77, 79, 89, 94, 95, 96, 98, 101, 103, 104, 105, 107, 112, 114
transfer payments, 31
transmission, 13, 14
transparency, 3, 54, 95, 96, 97
Treasury, 7, 31, 33, 34, 93
Treasury bills, 31
treatment, 95, 98
Troubled Asset Relief Program (TARP), viii, 88
turnover, 111

U

U.S. Department of the Treasury, 13, 16, 33, 38, 39, 40, 41, 42, 43
U.S. economy, vii, 2, 4
U.S. Treasury, 7, 12, 32, 33, 34, 40
UK, 18
unacceptable risk, 54
uniform, 25
unions, 36, 98

United, viii, 2, 3, 4, 5, 6, 8, 9, 10, 11, 16, 18, 20, 23, 25, 30, 36, 38, 42, 100, 109, 111
United Kingdom, 18, 38, 42, 109
United States, viii, 2, 3, 4, 5, 6, 8, 9, 10, 11, 16, 20, 23, 25, 30, 36, 42, 100, 109, 111
USA, 15
USA PATRIOT Act, 15

V

validation, 55, 56, 81, 85
valuation, 104
variables, 89, 90
volatility, 89, 98, 106
vote, 22, 23, 24, 25, 28
vulnerability, vii, 1

W

Washington, 3, 38, 39, 40, 41, 42, 43, 44, 75
weakness, viii, 88
web, 40
websites, 33
White Paper, 42
wholesale, 6, 9, 15, 39
World Bank, 43
worry, 91